# MESSAGES IN THE MALL

## Looking at Life
## in 600 Words or Less

# PAUL V. MARSHALL

# MESSAGES IN THE MALL

## Looking at Life in 600 Words or Less

### SEABURY BOOKS

*an imprint of Church Publishing Incorporated*
NEW YORK

Marshall, Paul Victor, 1947-
  Messages in the mall : looking at life in 600 words or less / Paul V. Marshall.
    p. cm.
  ISBN 978-1-59627-081-7 (pbk.)
    1. Christian life—Episcopal authors. I. Title.
BV4501.3.M2753 2008
277.3'0829—dc22

                                                              2007047210


Church Publishing Incorporated
445 Fifth Avenue
New York, NY 10016

www.churchpublishing.org


5  4  3  2  1

# FOR BILL LEWELLIS
*Father and Midwife*

# CONTENTS

# PREFACE

**N**OT OFTEN ENOUGH to give anyone a swelled head, but often enough to keep me at the keyboard, an adult being confirmed or received will tell me that they first came to the Episcopal Church because of my monthly columns in the secular papers. There is, of course, no way to know how many people have stayed away from the church for just the same reason! The offering of columns to some fifteen secular papers has been an attempt to get the word out: the Episcopal Church offers a unique way to be a Christian.

On the best months, columns have appeared in fifteen papers in the fourteen counties of the diocese. The average is nine. The series was begun at the urging of Canon Bill Lewellis, diocesan Communication Minister, who has a vision of a communicating church that the denomination as a whole is only beginning to grasp.

I offer these pieces as specimens, attempts to illustrate how a writer might engage a particular culture. I do not suggest that the content of these columns would be effective in other places.

The discipline to writing the columns has been to find an issue of general interest and make the connection to the Christian tradition in an Anglican way, and to do so within the six-hundred-word limit set by most papers. A few of the columns exceed that length, and were run as-is by the papers in consideration of our long relationship or because it was a slow news week. Six hundred words require focus and economy in writing. It is amazing how many adjectives one can learn to live without when the shade of an editor is looming. The most difficult part for a veteran preacher was to learn to write short paragraphs, at one to two sentences each, but I have often rejoined paragraphs here for ease of reading in book form.

These columns are almost always an intentional minority report in my part of the country, which explains why some themes occur so frequently and others seldom or never. They are written to provide a polite but direct alternative to an extraordinarily conservative religious and political culture. They attempt to offer good news particularly to those who cannot identify with or who have begun to question that culture, in either its protestant or Roman Catholic manifestations.

Given that most of the ink in the space allotted to religious columns in area newspapers is taken up by the dominant religious culture, I have from the first spent most of my time each month attempting to reach those who think Christianity is irrelevant or anti-intellectual, and those who have been burned by rigorist religion.

The repetition of themes, references, and even quotations over the decade is also based on the principles taught to us by successful advertising: the more you remind them, the more they remember. In addition, by way of contrast to the fundamentalism that dominates religion in this area, I often emphasize Jesus' provocative claim to himself *be* the truth, moving questions of truth to the arena of relationship with him and away from proof-texting.

Judaism comes up directly in a number of the columns, and is mentioned in very many of them. Bethlehem, Pennsylvania, styles itself the "Christmas City," a hard enough place to be a Jew, but Jews in our area particularly resent the fact that to the majority of local protestant writers they are nothing but a mission field. I have tried to address that concern directly, and also seek to make connections between Jewish and Christian thought without homogenizing them.

Although I have been more interested in building bridges, some columns involve controversy. Sometimes I have courted it; once it came entirely by surprise. The most gloves-off was a piece differing with the Lutheran Church–Missouri Synod after 9/11, "Godless Orthodoxy," which got a good deal of positive response from members of that church who were embarrassed by the overreaction of their leadership. The other column had consequences that I did not anticipate and still regret, as it was not intended to be controversial. It is "Mary, the Mother of Jesus," which still seems to me a most tactful and gentle explanation of why it might be useful to consider that Mary and Joseph had a normal married life after the birth of Jesus, as the Scriptures make plain. The Roman Catholic diocese of Scranton, part of my diocese, brought the full weight of its wrath down on one paper that carried my column in that overwhelmingly

Roman Catholic area, with the result that the paper has since that time carried no religious columns whatsoever! If I could have anticipated that degree of reactivity, I would not have written the piece—I quite literally died in Scranton, as the vaudevillians used to say.

Naturally, I would hope that these little pieces have some devotional use. In an age, however, when our church needs to seize every opportunity to get its message out, my fondest hope for this collection is that the reader will say, "Hey, I could do that at least as well as this guy"—and do so.

*+ PM*
*The Feast of All Saints, 2007*

# THE FIRST COLUMN, FEBRUARY 1997

## Bring on the Religious Voices . . . Please

A national newspaper editorialized about an American "moral vacuum" as it became clear that Newt Gingrich would be reprimanded for an ethics violation. Similar cries were briefly raised over the House banking scandal and the savings and loan bailout. A former mayor of New York can say, "I didn't commit a crime; I just didn't comply with the law." A former president claims, "If the president does it, it's not illegal." A hotel queen sneers, "Only little people pay taxes."

It is not hard to argue that America has no moral standards to speak of. From the permissiveness of thirty years ago, we have arrived at a point where it is considered downright rude to suggest to anyone that their personally chosen moral standards are discussable, much less in need of reexamination or correction. The assumption that desiring something implies a right to have it goes largely unchallenged.

Long after he had anything to gain by it, George Washington made an observation in his Farewell Address of 1796 that speaks to today's moral dilemma:

> Let us with caution indulge the supposition that morality can be maintained without religion. Whatever may be conceded to the influence of refined education on minds of peculiar structure, reason and experience both forbid us to expect that national morality can prevail in exclusion of religious principle.

The First Amendment, prohibiting government subsidy or special privilege for any religious group, was well in place when Washington spoke those words. We have trouble hearing them because in recent years freedom of religion has been replaced by a trend to suppress religious voices in public life. Legislation becomes suspect if a religious group is too strongly identified with it. One sometimes feels as though a moral position gotten from a fortune cookie will be more acceptable in public debate than one stemming from faith. "Let's not bring religion into it," rules out most of the moral and ethical thinking that has taken place in human history.

How our children are *not* taught about Martin Luther King Jr. offers a clear illustration of a near phobia about religion in our schools. Presentations of his life and work often speak of him as a civil rights leader, and that's all. Not mentioned is the fact that his speeches and writings show his ideas to spring from the content of his religious faith, and that the Southern Christian Leadership Conference in which he worked was a religious organization. King's particular style and emphases cannot be understood without understanding his religion. The same is true for Malcolm X, whose religious journey had a tremendous effect on his teaching.

This is not to suggest that religion in any of its forms has all the answers—something to try when we tire of thinking for ourselves. Quite the contrary, faith communities are meant to be safe and powerful places to test our thinking with people who share our starting point.

It also has to be admitted, of course, that like other movements, religion has helped to support, excuse, or ignore great evils. It has also been the inspiration of those who changed the world for the better, however, whether one looks to Martin Luther King or Mother Theresa. It is impossible to read the account in the Hebrew Scriptures of the creation of Israel and not wonder at the power of religious identity.

"Religion" means "that which binds." Religious thinking begins with the idea that people are bound to one another and to God, that life has connectedness, meaning, and purpose. People who believe they are bound to one another and to God have a different starting point when they consider morality. For them, a new factor is present in the equation from the beginning: responsibility to others.

# CHAPTER ONE
## Virtues and Vices

### Grace in an African Airport

Can lost luggage be an act of God? Do angels disguise themselves as porters? I do not know, but the possibilities are intriguing.

With my body screaming in several places after eighteen hours that are best left undescribed, I got off the plane in Johannesburg to find my main piece of luggage lost. Turtles are built for survival, not speed, and thus I do not travel light. In my carry-on I had only a partial change of clothes because of the room taken up by my other survival tools. I thought bitterly of the old joke about the Concorde: breakfast in Paris, lunch in New York, baggage in Bermuda.

Then the gift came in the form of a young man whose name tag said "Daniel." He zoomed in on my wounded and fretful appearance and offered to help me. Daniel spoke English, but in accents that were difficult for me to understand. I gave him a brisk "No, thank you" and moved on.

He followed me! This was not good news to a city boy. He persisted even when I dodged into a telephone area, only to discover that I had no idea how to work the South African telephone system. He cornered me and asked me somewhat urgently if I wouldn't please let him help me, as it was his job to help strangers. I started to realize how much I had mentally locked my car doors because Daniel was black. Like many other people of good will, I thought I had "gotten over" that.

Out of guilt I let him guide me to the shuttle bus, and found myself apologizing for my resistance on the grounds that I was upset that I had lost my luggage, was generally disoriented, and had never been to South Africa before. His response was odd. He shoved an open hand to me, almost at eye-level, and said something I could not understand, and said it again when I did not respond. I bent my head close to his, and he said very slowly for the third time (by the grace of God a rooster did not crow), "Wel-come." I took his hand gratefully.

It would have been enough if this were the end of it. For some strange reason the shuttle bus kept on not coming. This left us standing together, and we did what males of our species do instead of conversing: we asked each other questions. In response to something I asked he said, "If you are going to have a good visit in South Africa, you will have to be patient." I said, finally getting it, "Just like you've been patient with me?" Somehow proper grammar does not seem necessary during an epiphany.

In my first hour in the country I had been opened to experience and to human community when I had been focused on disorder and inconvenience. It took them four days to get my luggage to me. In the meantime, up in Swaziland I learned what it was like to wash out one's underwear each night, and what it is like to have "only" two shirts in places where some people feel fortunate to have one.

It is only as I write this that I remember that "Daniel" means "gift of God," a fact that may set the indoor record for slowness of perception. All of this took place as described, and perhaps gives us something to think about during the first Lent in what will be Africa's century.

## Maturity: The Accessible Virtue

I've always loved the title of the AARP magazine, *Modern Maturity*. It suggests an intangible aspect of having lived a few years that no hair dye commercial can approach. I am not in a position to comment on other religions but, every time *Modern Maturity* arrives, I wonder what a Christian magazine describing spiritual maturity would contain.

When St. Paul describes the virtues Christians should display as they share their gifts, he begins by saying that spiritual renewal, transformation of the mind, comes first: "Do not think of yourself more highly than you ought." In twenty-eight years of full-time church work I have never gotten used to Christians who get insulted. There is nothing more silly —or obscene—than a Christian with his or her nose out of joint! But it happens. I have no particularly immunity, either.

When it happens to me, I find myself wondering how someone like me, who follows an incarnate God who was spat upon, rejected by his own, beaten, and crucified, can ever feel insulted or insufficiently recognized. To feel that way, and to make it known, is the worst possible witness—it is a denial of Christ much worse than Peter's. Peter simply pretended not to know Jesus. The Christian with hurt feelings says to the world, yes, I know the crucified Messiah, but I don't think he's worth following at the risk of having my feeling tweaked. Well, we all know that temptation—it's why, to use St. Paul's words, our minds need transforming.

A very useful definition of neurosis is a fixation on one's worth in comparison with others. Thus, if others are praised, the neurotic feels put down or slighted. Gore Vidal once put it this way: "It is not enough to succeed—others must fail." That is perhaps a little strong but it does reflect much of the attitude of those who feel slighted, however briefly, when others are in the limelight.

Such an attitude can seriously hamper the witness and mission of any religious organization. The personal consequences are quite high also. Whenever we are seriously worried about questions of status or recognition among Jesus' disciples, the evil one has got us. "If you belonged to the world, the world would love you as its own," Jesus said. "You do not belong to the world, but I have chosen you out of the world—therefore the world hates you. Remember the word that I said to you, 'Servants are not greater than their master.' If they persecuted me, they will persecute you."

I do not necessarily recommend the movie *The Devil's Advocate*, but the closing scene is unforgettable. Our hero finally does the right thing—the principled thing—and then when a reporter seeks him out to suggest an interview about this, he begins to feel special about being raised up for admiration. Immediately there is a close-up of Satan, Al Pacino, who looks right into the camera and says, each syllable a dagger of ice, "Vanity is still my favorite sin." End of movie.

The reason St. Paul puts the reminder about pride at the beginning of his long list of Church virtues is that as long as we keep that sin at bay, the great things can flourish. Put positively, as long as we keep Christ's attitude of self-giving as the measure of each of our motives and actions, we will in fact be transformed by the renewal of our minds. All those other gifts will have the space and light they need to grow—a good start toward eternal maturity.

## Pride Is a Silly Thing to Die For

My wife is shoveling snow. I've been struggling with a respiratory problem and it would be insanity to join her. I know this, yet guilt and anxiety are with me, despite the fact that she is not showing any signs of martyrdom or self-sacrifice.

There's this guy thing: the heavy lifting is my domain. Navigating our steep, twisting driveway with my enormous snowblower is the one place I still get to be the pioneer, making the cave safe and accessible. Instead of hearing the roar and inhaling the exhaust of the engine, I type this to the scrape-scrape of a patient and relentless woman's unceasing efforts with a shovel. It's embarrassing.

Few of us are good at doing the work of being sick, especially when the sickness is not dramatic or life threatening, just boring and frustrating. Staying still, being intentionally quiet, adopting the discipline of rest. They go against the grain for those who enjoy being productive.

The forced downtime reminds me of how little rest most of us build into our lives. The question occurs to me with new emphasis. Perhaps rest and recreation are like investing for retirement—which you need to do intentionally over the long haul to get the benefits. The religious word for this is stewardship, management of resources with a goal in mind.

Then there is control. Not being able to organize and administer one's life and work because of physical weakness is too clear a reminder that in the end we will have to give up absolutely everything. The usual ability to be active, to be in charge of one's life, enables us to deny that each of us is living on borrowed time. I now have enough relatives and friends nearing life's end for this thought to be uncomfortable. My turn will come. Let's change the subject.

I am fascinated by the recent revelation that Prince Charles has a man who uses a golden key to squeeze out the prince's toothpaste for him every morning. Being waited on when one is well and in charge is an experience of power. Being waited on to that extent must make one feel, well, royal.

Being waited on when one is weak and vulnerable is not so pleasant, but it does bring a choice. It can be an experience of frustration, defeat, and humiliation or an experience of grace. That slippery word means receiving what we are not entitled to because somebody is kind. One can either get tired of having to say thank you, or one can learn to cherish each opportunity for acknowledging human kindness. When she comes back in, I will try the latter path.

One of the reasons Christianity is challenging is that it involves the concept of a savior, someone who does for us what we cannot do for ourselves. For most of us it seems un-American to step outside the circle of self-reliance, of self-actualization, of paying one's own way—in this country being bailed out by the government is for the very rich and to some extent for the very poor. We in the middle are used to taking care of ourselves. To have to accept the fact that we need someone to show us how to live and how to die puts us precisely where I am with my snow-shoveling wife.

So I find that the choice in attitude I make about the snow shoveling is a measure of my attitude toward the big things of life. Pride is a very silly thing to die for. Will I allow myself to be cared for and be genuinely grateful for that care, or will I resist the grace that is offered me?

## Accepting Responsibility Leads to Life

Two people covered with leaves sit in the back of an open convertible driven by a man with a long white beard. The drawing is a child's depiction of God driving Adam and Eve out of paradise.

The ancient story evokes mixed reactions. Some of its themes are not so helpful, as when humanity's fear of snakes, the pain of childbirth, and the domination of women by men, and the sweat and blood it can take just to stay alive, are explained in terms of the tale of the garden.

There is a lesson in the ancient story about the difference between shame and guilt. What if Adam and Eve had said, "Yes, we betrayed your trust. We accept responsibility and hope we can resume our relationship." The Bible may have been reduced to twelve pages entitled, "Paradise Retained."

As the story goes, Adam strayed from appropriate guilt, which can become the occasion of grace, into shame that feels exposed and protects itself with flimsy fig leaves of evasion and passing the buck. Nothing graceful can happen when I deny, rationalize, or defend against my guilt. There can be no forgiveness and reconciliation. There can never be learning from mistakes I insist I didn't make.

The most important thing we can ever say to our children is, "I was wrong; I'm sorry, and I hope you will forgive me." I cringe when people who carry unresolved hurts from their childhood say, somewhat mechanically and with little conviction, "Well, my parents did the best they could." That is simply not true. Every parent knows times we put ourselves first and let our children down. Where guilt is accepted, however, grace can happen. How much different to say, "My parents made mistakes, and sometimes they hurt me. I know that I bear that pain still, and I choose to forgive them."

The inability to accept personal responsibility plagues our society. Suppose the allegations brought against Clarence Thomas were true and he had simply said, "Yes, in a very different culture, I made remarks that I now know were simply wrong. I know better now, and apologize to anyone I offended or hurt." It would have been the shortest confirmation process in history.

The world is generally not prepared to deal with adults who take responsibility for what they've done, make restitution where they can, and move on in grace. Responsible adults don't look for deniability.

This notion of adult responsibility appears again in the gospel story—this time from the point of view of maturity and health—when Jesus' family, for whatever reason, wants him to stop being, well, so weird and embarrassing, and come home. Jesus counters that his true family are those who seek to know and do God's will.

There comes a time in each of our lives—perhaps more than one time—when we choose no longer to live under the protective umbrella of letting our parents or anyone else say what is true, good, or desirable for us. Though we never stop loving our parents, we build close relationships with those who share our own beliefs and values and work to implement them.

The Christian claims that the relationship with God—which Adam and Eve forgot as they started dodging responsibility—is restored in Jesus Christ. Life in Christ's Church is meant to be life in a kind of garden, with many kinds of nourishment available for the picking. All it takes to go back there—to go forward there—is to accept the gift that comes to those who will own who they are and accept what God will give them as they walk the earth in relationship with their Creator.

## Embracing Necessary Pain

Next to my wife, Diana, the most important person in my life recently has been Jeff. When I am with him, I experience deep, prolonged, and burning pain. The pain is necessary. Without the brutal physical therapy that follows the repair of a massive tear in the shoulder muscles and some carpentry on the bones themselves, my shoulder would quickly freeze, and my arm would be almost useless.

Jeff dislikes hurting people. He knows, though, that unless he does his job ruthlessly I will be a cripple. He has a goal in mind, so he moves my muscles and tendons, painful as that is. I owe him a great deal for that pain.

More ordinary suffering is at times also necessary. It, too, is a gift. When I was a child, my mother diligently sat for three years and made me practice the piano until the spark caught. I will never be a very good musician, but I owe her for suffering through those sessions—and through my attempts at avoidance—to give me access to the great joy of making music. I could not even imagine that joy at the age of nine. All I knew was my suffering, with no clue to hers until my turn came as a parent and I failed to carry the torch.

We Baby Boomers were generally not fond of discipline. Our children are paying for it. They pay in their ignorance of Western culture, in the lasting trauma of homes broken because spouses simply stopped trying to be faithful, and in a general sense of instability.

Christianity's claim that God knew suffering seemed outrageous in the first century. In the world of the Greeks and Romans, it was characteristic of a god to be beyond suffering. Imagine the reaction to a religion that spoke of God on the move, taking on all the limitations and vulnerabilities of human life, then going on to experience the most hideous form of death the word knew, emerging the victor. How absurd that a suffering god from the backwoods of civilization should have anything to offer a sophisticated world!

We live in a culture almost as sophisticated as that of the first century. Like its inhabitants, we stumble on questions of suffering, pain, the mystery of evil, and the even greater mystery of human cruelty. In the midst of that predicament, what use is the suffering of God? The New Testament witnesses to several aspects of the cross. Most basic is the gospel message that when we see the love God poured out in the face of our evil, we are convicted and also experience forgiveness.

There is more. God suffers with the world, showing it the eternal moment of the crucifixion, always offering the path of growth where we prefer death, always waiting for us to mature. The path to maturity requires the mastery of self, the pain of discipline.

It is not surprising then that there are places in the New Testament that tell Jesus' story in terms of disciplined pursuit of a goal. The Letter to the Hebrews is particularly blunt. Jesus is spoken of in dynamic terms, the "pioneer and perfecter of our faith." The Lamb is also a tiger. Jesus' suffering has a purpose: "who for the sake of the joy that was set before him endured the cross, disregarding its shame."

To mature spiritually means, in part, having the nerve to suffer. We do it with the support of community, word, and sacraments, but the choice to embrace necessary pain is something that only an individual can make. Each day offers the chance to be a hero.

---

## Encouragement, Curiosity, and Cutting Slack

Along with its promises of everlasting life, religion has great practical value for the here and now. Religious practices should make us stronger, better, kinder—and less of a pain in the neck to those around us.

*How* to integrate religious ideals with day-to-day life has challenged us from Cain and Abel on. How does one get transformed? The answers are many and varied. For many of us, the deliberate and intentional practice of virtues we may not have made fully our own is how we get them into our hearts and heads. People in some recovery programs say bring the body and the mind will follow.

It is by setting certain goals and working to *live into* them that we find ourselves to have changed. This was brought home to me several years ago by a friend called Peter.

Peter and I were among the faculty leading a large group of students and alumni on a tour of England. During long bus trips over back roads, many on board got carsick. Peter has good sea legs. He made his way to the little galley in the bus and brought bouillon, coffee, and tea to people who wouldn't risk leaving their seats.

Peter began in a lighthearted way to speak of his "coffee ministry," an expression that would have been merely cute in other circumstances. His person and his genuineness, however, had a profound effect on the group. Soon we had many "ministries" going as people found small ways to help one another. A simple act had transformed weary travelers into a community.

I suggest here three simple "ministries" that could become a part of our dealing with one another. They can bring transformation to those who give and receive them.

### The Ministry of Encouragement

Taking the time to notice people, to thank them for what they do, can change the nature of an organization. Do you ever just call someone, perhaps a colleague or a fellow volunteer, to tell them they are doing a great job or that you appreciated what they said at a meeting or a gathering? It will change both of you.

### The Ministry of Curiosity

I can count on the thumbs of one hand the number of times someone has seen something I've said or written on a controversial subject and called or written me to ask why I said it, rather than just firing off a salvo that usually did not help matters. How different to say "My, that's a different way to approach this; how did you come to that conclusion?" By asking a question instead of attacking, instead of putting the other person on the defensive, you have started a conversation.

### The Ministry of Cutting Slack

Almost nobody gets up in the morning determined to be your enemy, or to ruin your day. If something sounds different or potentially alienating, why not remember that communication is a complex process. For example, almost no two people share exactly the same sense of humor. Instead of getting under your skin, the other person may be trying to amuse you. Also, as the nation becomes increasingly multicultural, it is helpful to remember that different cultures have different ideas of what it means to be polite.

This third ministry might also be called the ministry of not taking offense when none is intended. It does not come easily to minds trained for critical thinking, but finding the best possible explanation for the words of others is a virtue. Practicing it spares two people a fight, and may change them as well.

## Overcoming Perfection(ism)

If something is worth doing, it's worth doing badly. Late in my college years I accepted the fact that, although I played well enough, I did not have what it takes to be a full-time professional musician. I continued to practice and play the organ from 1969 until 1988. Then I stopped dead.

I had taken a teaching job at Yale and was associated, through an inter-disciplinary program, with the performance faculty in the School of Music. Surrounded by excellence, I could not stand to hear myself play. I sold the small organ we had in our home, and devoted myself to my computer's keyboard, playing in a kind of mental game show I called *Typing for Tenure*. While the satisfactions of research and writing are real, they are not music. Though I would occasionally play the piano—it is not an instrument for which I have passion—that did not really count.

There are, I think, other perfectionists in the world who join me in not doing what they cannot do perfectly. You see them throwing golf clubs across the fairway and stomping away or not joining in some group activities or generally "hiding their light under a bushel." Do you know people who have given up swimming because they look middle-aged in a bathing suit?

Late last fall, I made an offhand remark about looking for a used organ. From that time I found myself playing more and more. I have come to terms with the fact that at nearly fifty-five I cannot play half so well as I could at twenty, and that I will not have the time to practice seriously this side of retirement. I have wrestled with the part of me that adopted the perfectionist theme in my family history. I have wrestled with the ghost of my organ teacher, a man so driven that he would terminate a lesson if more than one wrong note was played.

Defeating the perfectionist ghost has not been easy; nor is it complete. It involves remembering that I am playing for myself, not for an audience of critics. It means focusing on the beauty of the music, the genius of the composer, and the sound of the instrument. It is like walking through a gallery of pictures one could never paint: seeing beauty in one canvas makes you continue the walk to the others. It means settling for what are only occasional moments of artistry in long sessions of mediocrity.

Enjoying the structure of the music, appreciating the creativity of the composer, and occasionally playing in a way that sounds "right," are rewarding enough to displace insistence that it be done right or not done at all. Maybe that is why they call it playing.

I am not warning you to avoid my street in the early evening for the sake of your ears. My point is what St. Paul said: "Having gifts that differ, let us use them." My question is, what have we missed because we have not dared to be less than the best? Can perfectionism be a sin?

It is not just about playing. I know people who do not practice a profession for which they were trained because they cannot be the best at it. I know people who were told once that they aren't creative or funny or competent in some field or another. Because they believed it, their lives have been impoverished.

My fellow mediocrities, let's enjoy the gifts we have been given—no matter how modest we may think them to be.

---

## Being Pleasant

Of the celebrities who died in recent years, I most miss James Stewart. There was a wonderful consonance in who he was and most of the parts he played: kindly yet nobody's fool, highly principled but never a prude, a patriot who was not a chauvinist. His last appearance in a film was in 1983, but even after he retired, it felt good to know that he was out there. Two memories of his work occur to me, because he gave credibility to his lines from a place deep inside him.

In *The Philadelphia Story*, Tracy (Katharine Hepburn) is afraid of what may have occurred when she and Mike (Stewart) were drinking on the previous night, especially as she has found his watch in her bedroom. When he tells her that nothing happened, she then wonders if he found her unattractive or forbidding. Probably no other actor could bring off Stewart's line, as he notes that she was drunk and unpretentiously adds: "There are rules about that."

In the Cole Porter musical remake, *High Society* (wonderful in its own way), this scene falls apart completely. Frank Sinatra simply could not put this line across, and even looks a little embarrassed as he tries. Grace Kelly seems to recognize a hopeless situation, and delivers the setup lines very badly indeed.

"There are rules about that." In a culture in search of character, Stewart's easy congruence in claiming the priority of principles over self-gratification is a gentle invitation to ask ourselves whether or not principles guide our decision making. It is worth noting that during World War II he did not entertain American forces—he volunteered to be part of them.

The bit of dialogue that moves me the most, however, is Stewart's delivery of Elwood P. Dowd's observations in *Harvey*. Dowd is courteous to everyone he meets, and is notorious for inviting strangers to eat with him. He is never deterred by the unkindness or scorn of others. When questioned about this, he observes, "Years ago, my mother used to say to me, she said, 'In this world, Elwood'—she always used to call me Elwood—'In this world, Elwood, you must be oh, so smart, or oh, so pleasant.' Well, for years I was smart. I recommend pleasant. You may quote me."

Smart or pleasant? Dowd's transition from smart to pleasant reflects a principle: there will not be significant change in the world until we all put energy into becoming better people. But in enjoying Dowd's contrast of smart and pleasant, we can remember that the central truth of Christianity is not the wisdom or the power of God, but God's taking flesh, coming near to be with us, vulnerable to us at our most unpleasant, and triumphing over death itself.

In the Sermon on the Mount, Jesus teaches that the meek are blessed—and this is so not because they are wimps or unsmart, for they are not (and the word Jesus used doesn't mean that), but because the meek heroically choose to sweeten life rather than manipulate it. So trying to be "oh, so pleasant" is not to imitate Little Mary Sunshine. It is adopting an important discipline. In a New Testament letter of John we read that if we do not love people whom we can see, we cannot claim to love the God whom we cannot see.

This teaching raises being "pleasant" to a new plateau: love for God is expressed, at least in part, in love for one another. It also suggests that people who seek to be happy may find that the path to daily happiness is not hard to find or follow. That is, it says to those who are tired of or suspicious of the daily battle to be "oh, so smart" that there is an easily accessible alternative.

## Accepting Consequences

The prophet Hosea spoke of those who sow the wind and reap the whirlwind. Humorist Will Rogers said that religious people sow wild oats six days a week, and, on the seventh day, pray for crop failure. Whether we prefer the stern or gentler version, there does seem to be something in the religious mind that seeks to suspend cause and effect, or at least to change the odds.

There is a story about Jesus being tempted in the wilderness. The last of those temptations is to jump off a tower to demonstrate that God really would take care of him. His response: you should not tempt the Lord your God.

I have heard and thought about this passage many ways over the years. We often do, individually and corporately, tempt God or tempt fate, however one puts it. Then when the ax falls, we feel that God has let us down by not protecting us from the consequences of our behavior.

Philosophers and religious thinkers know that every system breaks down a bit when trying to account for evil and random suffering. There is nonetheless reason to consider how much cause and effect rather than a vengeful God are at the root of some of our problems.

I am not making this up: I have sat at the bedside of a person who smoked heavily for more than thirty years and wept about his lung cancer, "Why did God do this to me?" I have myself been a person who indulged in carbohydrates (especially Oreos) immoderately and wondered why I was "stricken" with adult-onset diabetes.

If we abuse our bodies, they will rebel. If we neglect our children, their personalities may well form in ways that disconcert us. If we do not work daily on prayer and spiritual practices, when crisis comes we may well perceive nothing but emptiness. It isn't vengeance; it's the way things work.

If this is true on the individual level, one cannot but ask if it is true on the societal level. The prophets of Israel tried to warn their contemporaries that their aggressively two-class society would bring only doom. As the distance between the haves and have-nots widens in America, do we assume to think that we have a special status that will protect us from the same results?

Biblical prophets were killed for saying this sort of thing. People who say it today are simply made fun of. Neither method of disposing of the messenger prevents results. Nonetheless, behaviors have consequences. Religious people might well ask themselves if they are expecting to be excused from the laws of cause and effect with regard to how they treat their bodies, their loved ones, and society.

Think of the tremendous forces one must overcome just to change one's eating or smoking or exercise habits. How many times must one multiply that to get an idea of the amount of resistance a political system has to righting wrongs from which people profit? It makes sense to acknowledge that only those who have the insight and the persistence to regulate themselves will be able to orchestrate change on any larger level. Nobody loses weight or builds muscles just by being angry at their fat or their puniness. People who want to change must take responsibility for a plan that they follow with a kind of ruthlessness.

The New Testament says that we look to Jesus in part because "he was tempted in every way as we are, but did not sin." Jesus did not presume on his status with God; he did not jump off the tower. Neither ought we to take foolish chances assuming that God will rescue us from our own behavior.

## Is Telling the Truth Irrelevant?

Super Bowl Sunday never was the time of "the highest incidence" of domestic violence. It is not even a time of a particularly high rate of violence. When pressed, the women's magazine that claimed this baseless untruth a few years ago defended itself by saying that, even though this was in fact a deliberate lie, it made what the editors considered to be an important point.

Recently, when a *New York Times* reporter was exposed as a plagiarist and liar, journalists investigating the story met a stone wall: the publisher and editors of the nation's paper of record repeatedly refused to speak to the press about their employee's behavior and the policies that protected him.

The irony was delicious, the hypocrisy profound.

Anyone deposed in legal proceedings may encounter questioners who can distort a situation by the "yes or no" questions they ask, ripping events or facts out of the context that gives them their meaning. How people who deceive for a living and give their honorable profession a bad name can sleep at night puzzles me; it must be all the money.

We are being treated to self-righteous arguments on strictly party lines again in Washington, about who was telling what truth about Iraq, and are apparently expected to ignore the fact that both sides know an election is coming.

Truth is too important to be defined by politicians or the press. A politician has the mission of maintaining power and a newspaper is in the business of selling papers—neither is motivated to take the unsensational, complicated, or embarrassing path that the whole truth usually involves. As a consequence, truth suffers when the teller stands to lose money or clout. Truth disappears when "facts" are assembled to distort or distract, when an advocate's commitment to zealous representation becomes an exercise in misdirection and deception.

Essentially dishonest behavior has been defended by a deceptive appeal to principle or a piece of irrelevant data that only makes the original lie worse. Nobody was deceived when an archbishop claimed that priests were independent contractors not under his control. The contempt for the public displayed in such lying is depressing, however.

Because we live in the age of spin, the age of the misleading sound bite, the age where perception is valued more than accuracy, it is perhaps no wonder that young people increasingly find discussion of truth telling irrelevant or hopelessly antiquated.

Whether one is Christian on not, there is something to be learned from Jesus' claim in John's Gospel, "I am the truth." Beyond mere questions of getting data right, how one assembles and uses information is ultimately tested by the relationships among people. Jesus later claims that knowing him was to know the truth that sets free.

Data and "factoids" assembled to manipulate, evade, or alienate are not truth, because they defile human relationships. They may be legal, but they are certainly immoral. On the other hand, when we accurately report things that are difficult, complex, and perhaps unexciting, in a way that builds relationships and emphasizes the value of human beings, we are telling truth. When we report what is wrong in order to make it right, we are telling truth.

My cousins the Lutherans used to teach their children that part of truth telling is to "put the best construction on everything." Here is religion at its most dangerous: if we all did that, our humanity would thrive.

## The Importance of Pulling Weeds

I have a grudging admiration for weeds. They are hearty and prolific. If someone sneezes near a dandelion in Duluth, I have the little yellow darlings in my Bethlehem lawn the next week. One little weed left untended can take over a plot of earth. Such a small plant, just doing what comes naturally, can provide lower back pain and aching knees for thousands of gardeners.

What makes any given plant a weed depends, of course, on what you do and do not want to grow in a given space. No matter how beautiful or how greatly valued elsewhere, if the plant is choking out what you are depending on for food or money or simple delight, it is a weed.

Building and nurturing community—relationships with common purpose and common support—is very much like planting and nurturing a garden. Just a few weeds, if not attended to, can kill what you are trying to grow. Like the weeds in a real garden, if considered alone, they are just healthy plants; in the context of the garden they are killers.

One of these hearty perennials is accidental bomb throwing. Though done by a person of perfectly good will with the best of intentions—that is often the problem—bombing a positive conversation with an emotionally charged issue inevitably brings the potential creativity of the conversation to a screeching halt. None of the hoped-for results of the conversation are achieved. Nor is understanding of the injected issue advanced. The power of the emotionally charged issue simply drives out everything around it.

More depressing still is the release of negativity that all too clearly gives speakers a sense of power—and a free ride. If challenged about raining on other people's parades, they can reply that they were just expressing their feelings and ideas. How often has "just telling the truth" or "what I'm feeling" done irreparable harm?

Anybody is able to report the data or express their feelings. Community builders, however, know the wisdom of the New Testament injunction to speak the truth in love.

Love here is not the emotional attachment that makes people tell their beloved that yes, their new hairstyle does look good. Love in this context is the carefully examined concern for how things will turn out for the health of the community as a whole—and, on that basis, some reasonable determination of how much truth to tell at any given time.

Jesus once told his disciples that he had many more things to tell them, but that they could not bear to hear all of it at once. Just as we do not teach children subtraction and long division on the same day, community builders ask if the community can process more truth at any given moment; on that basis, they decide what to say and when to say it.

As we speak strongly held opinions or feelings, then, it is important to look at the garden in which one speaks. Am I planting a rose or a weed in this community? For the health of the community, one's motives are not nearly so important as results.

The larger challenge to any community is to take a stand about weeds. If we don't stand up to dandelions, the lawn will be gone. Often people in communities or organizations that center on doing good have difficulty saying no to the weeds that clog their progress lest someone's feelings be hurt. Perhaps the next time someone sidetracks progress in our group, we might think of our lawns and politely but firmly say no.

## Patient Prophecy in an Elevator

On one of last month's coldest days, my friend stepped into an elevator with a woman who was shivering. Bill gave her a sympathetic look. "I pity the people who have to work outdoors today," she said. "Yes, and those who have to live outdoors," he replied. Silence. To the seventh floor. As the doors opened she quipped, "They could get jobs if they wanted to." Then, she hurried out of the car.

I have field-tested this true story. At first hearing people respond as I initially did, somewhat disapproving. Something else may have been going on. Bill's few concerned words about the homeless had clearly gotten under her skin. She had been thinking.

The beginning of compassion is dealing with ourselves, with our resistance to thinking and acting outside of what is comfortable to us. I think she began to do that thinking, and was doing so because of how little Bill said. He gave her room to think. Her defensive response suggests she was doing so. I'm willing to accept the possibility that the next day she made a contribution to the Allentown Rescue Mission.

I don't know if Bill's remarks were inspired or "just" highly intuitive. The story, however, is a reminder that there is more than one way to be a prophet, one who speaks for God. Ephesians 4 enjoins us to "speak the truth in love." Each of us is aware of when we were or were not motivated entirely by love when we spoke, and of times when one love seemed to require rejecting another love when speaking.

I think here, however, about "speaking the truth." How much is enough? Should Bill have preached her a sermon on social concerns, Jesus' absolute preference for the poor, or the overwhelming concern of both Testaments for economic justice? Ought he to carry tracts with him explaining Christian compassion?

Well, there are occasions when those tactics could be perfect, and I have some pictures of Africa I'd like to show you. I would also like to show you some statistics about life in parts of Pennsylvania. This year, the entire church is following Luke's Gospel, where we deal repeatedly with Jesus' own critique of greed and exclusion. As a church, we could investigate the Scriptures more thoroughly and more often.

We know the saying that if the only tool you have is a hammer, every problem appears to be a nail. Bill's story is a reminder that there is more than one tool in our kit as we witness, teach, or even preach. Sometimes it is important to inform. Sometimes it is important to persuade. Sometimes it is important to invite people to think new thoughts. It takes gifts to do any of these, but as I write this I admire (and envy) those who do provoke thought with just a few words.

The "prophet" in the elevator was patient. The patient prophet has to overcome the need for instant closure, decision, or results. Such patience is not to be mistaken for a lack of concern or urgency. It simply recognizes and respects the varying rates at which individuals grow. My friend's witness reminds me that the Spirit has worked in many of our lives gradually and progressively, assisted by the patient words of others.

One other thing. What if Bill had chosen simply to nod in agreement with the lady's doubtlessly kind observation about the people working outside? Subtle, patient prophets teach us courage, too.

## On Eating Together

We find pleasure and meaning in eating together. Many books have been written about how, when, why, and what we eat when we have meals together. Meals have meaning. At times, that meaning has to be repaired.

I know of a troubled family who went to a family therapist and poured out their seemingly endless concerns. The therapist told them to come back in sixty days; in the meantime, on each of those days, they were to have at least one meal with all family members present.

They were desperate enough to change a few schedules, give up a few sports practices, and alter the commute in order to try to eat together. With great effort, they missed only a few meals. It was no miracle cure: eating together made them deal with one another, made them name some of their problems, and provoked long encounters between various members of the family outside of mealtime. But coming together at least once a day at a time when they were nourished together changed the context in which their relationship took place.

All members of the family were struck by one event that seemed to change their expectations about this process. About halfway into the experiment, the night came when they laughed together. It took them by surprise, was a bit embarrassing, and took some getting used to. The more that happened, though, the better they felt. They had bonded again.

Unfortunately, this is not a fairy tale, so the happy ending has not come yet. Their problems were not gone, but they had become a community again. Eating together, or better, not eating alone, was changing how they understood themselves. It made them realize that coming to the table was healthy. Even if they had stomped out of a room a few hours before, a meal they had to attend provided reentry into the family.

In the Midwest, Germans still have a saying, "gesegnete Mahlzeit," a wish for a "blessed meal time." Jews have a whole body of worship activities that sanctifies the family meal, particularly on Friday, as sundown brings the Sabbath.

In general, world religions and local tribal rites express the nature of eating, especially of eating together, with toasts, prayers, and dances. These may be elaborate or quite simple. The shortest prayer in my tradition is: "Bless this food to our use, and us to your service, and keep us always mindful of the needs of others."

Saying a prayer of thanks before meals—"grace" is from the Latin for "thanks"—recognizes in the food our interdependence with the creation and with one another. Grace before meals acknowledges also that we depend on the Giver of all things.

A few seconds spent in thankful prayer are not much, but cumulatively this habit forms our attitudes toward life, the universe, and everything. Table prayers are not just for children. Real men say grace. Real women have always known this.

In this way, the meals we share call us out of isolation and out of the illusion of self-sufficiency. Meals can create a time and a place where we meet with an awareness of being sustained by the same thing, a time and a place where we can laugh. In our meals we can understand ourselves to be recipients of the gift of community, a base from which to serve the world, to share food with those who are hungry, to share life with those we love.

## Conflict Advances Truth

Have you ever tried to discuss an idea and, after mentioning that you disagree with what someone has proposed, been told that the proposer is a good person? This emotional blackmail is meant to end the discussion rather than risk a conversation.

All religious groups I know about seem to have many people who are afraid of conflict. They cannot distinguish in their minds between disagreement and condemnation. Afraid to say "no," they live with things they cannot agree with or do jobs they do not really want to do. One day they explode. Then the situation often cannot be repaired, and the group has a problem that may take years to overcome, if it can be overcome.

Because people are afraid of conflict, religious institutions and community groups often tolerate behavior that would be unacceptable at any other level of society.

I have been aware of people storming out of meetings after committing atrocious behavior, and the rest of the group then nervously wondering how they could get the offender back. Such groups operate with the unspoken belief that if they stand up against bad behavior and for their basic principles, they will not survive. The opposite, in fact, is true. One compromise leads to another, and their major goals are missed altogether, because there is no backbone in the organism.

There is no law against conflict in either the Hebrew or Christian Scriptures. Rather than encouraging silence, the New Testament urges readers to "speak the truth in love." The prophets in Israel pulled no punches. Jesus is not remembered as just going along with things for the sake of apparent peace. In fact, the gospels have him on one occasion more or less "disowning" his mother and brothers and sisters when they tried to stop him from disturbing the public mind.

There is nothing wrong with saying, "I think you did the wrong thing," or, "Where I disagree with you is. . . ." (It is often helpful to ask a question first, however!)

There is everything wrong with saying, "Because you did such and such, you are stupid, worthless, etc." My complaint about most of the talk show hosts I hear on the radio, whether liberal or conservative, is that they poison the American mind. Rather than just disagreeing about facts and their interpretation, they dismiss the intelligence or emotional stability of the other side. This is entertaining but destructive of conversation.

Why does no one criticize political spending in terms of the number of mouths it could feed? I dread every major election year because political parties spend fortunes to keep the American public from discussing basic issues objectively. To do so would be to admit that each party has some truth behind its platform, and that nobody operates without self-interest of one kind or another.

Conflict—disagreement discussed thoroughly and fairly—is the primary means of advancing the truth. Careful listening and thoughtful response advance common understanding and progress. Conflict that is kept on the level of ideas but does not discuss personalities is a sign of health, of thinking.

That some political and religious movements teach people not to think is a burden that diminishes every culture. Even in an age when it seems that "sensitivity" remains the highest virtue, it is no sin to disagree vigorously with an idea or someone's perception of events.

On the other hand, perhaps it is a sin to confuse being valuable with being right. Surely, no one is always right! The first sign of healthy humility is the ability to be taught. Conflict without nastiness, then, may be the most caring path of all.

## Of Frogs and Sailors

A young woman encountered a talking frog. "O please, fair maiden, help me. I am really a handsome and rich prince. If you kiss me, I will return to that state, and you can marry me, and cook and clean for me and have my children, all under the direction of my mother." She did not accept the frog's offer. Later that day she remarked to herself how much, indeed, the frog's legs did taste like chicken.

This story found on the Internet expresses the trap of human life. The woman was right to be outraged—even to drop the frog back in the middle of the pond scum to make her point. But to kill and eat him?

Each of us has our list of grievances: some real, unjust, and outrageous things we have suffered; others, imagined. It's too easy to believe, however, that our list justifies our doing harm to others. We've all seen people so obsessed with outrage that they believe their anger is proof they are right to be miserable and to make others so. We also know, and sometimes are, people who have on blinders about how we offend or oppress, and how we profit by systems that crush others.

In the midst of peevishness that flares into feuds, in the midst of willingness to exploit and oppress, in the midst of willingness to think that justice implies or excuses revenge, God set up the cross of Jesus Christ.

The world's destiny revolves around a person with no power in the ordinary way, no real estate, no money. Jesus' only power was the truth of his words, the integrity of his life, and the compassion of his signs and miracles.

From that base of moral power, he invited people to new life. In the earliest gospel, Mark, Jesus' first sermon was simply, "Repent and believe the gospel." Turn from what destroys you and others, and live a life where all are valued but none are privileged, where giving is more valued than receiving, where many come from the East and the West to sit at table together under the reign of God.

For the sake of the frog—still in each of us—yearning to be free and beautiful; for the sake of those who need to throw off oppression by killing and eating the oppressor; for the sake of the world God loves; may we gear our imaginations to pray our way into the New Testament paradox about living through dying as expressed in the concluding lines of a prayer said to come from St. Francis:

> Grant that we may not so much seek to be consoled as to console; to be understood as to understand; to be loved as to love. For it is in giving that we receive; it is in pardoning that we are pardoned; and it is in dying that we are born to eternal life.

Contemporary artists who penetrate reality with their art can also help us. A verse of "Suzanne," a song of the 1960s by Leonard Cohen, suggests there was something more to Jesus than a quick or literal reading of the Bible uncovers. (Water is used in the song, as in the Bible, to mean the tide that sweeps over us, the waters of death.)

> And Jesus was a sailor
> When he walked upon the water
> And he spent a long time watching
> From his lonely wooden tower
> And when he knew for certain
> Only drowning men could see him

He said "All men will be sailors then
Until the sea shall free them."

---

## What's That Funny Smell?

The French say that if you smell the same bad smell in three different places, it's you.

On sabbatical a couple of years ago I lived on a ship for nine weeks among twenty-seven hundred people whom I had never seen before and with whom I had no professional or personal connection—a completely blank slate. You can imagine my surprise when some familiar stresses appeared in a few of those new relationships. Other people were not having those problems in the same situations; but some, to be sure, had other conflicts.

Haunted by the French proverb, I began carefully monitoring my responses to people around me. I also sharpened my people-watching skills, looking for clues as others experienced their big and small stresses in that temporary community of strangers. (The bloody fistfight between two women in the laundry room was probably the classic moment.)

It was a reminder that people will always be people; wherever we go, there will be stimuli to which we may react with aggression, anger, irritation, or hurt. Each response is a choice we made long ago, and is now so ingrained and automatic that it seems like a "feeling." The problem is about us, not about those who stimulate us in ways we don't like.

Constant monitoring of one's perceptions and reactions can be a big task, complicated for religious people when the person to whom we react in a bad-smelling way is actually in the wrong. Religion is very much about how to live, and that characteristic includes beliefs about right and wrong, clean and unclean, in and out. The clear violation of clear standards can trigger bad-smelling reactions that hurt our souls more than they set situations straight.

Part of the problem is that the many religious traditions generally endorse more than one model for the word "justice." Some of us retain the message that justice restores: it puts things right and sets individuals on a path to healing. Some of us retain the message that justice is about revenge, that things cannot be right until someone has been shamed and perhaps punished.

Focusing on revenge and shame is quite different from insisting on accountability, which I entirely endorse personally and also in the criminal justice system. My concern here, however, is with the heart. The need for revenge and punishment has to be carefully watched, especially when we disguise it. We have all scoffed at public figures whose various crusades betray their own needs to punish, avenge, and accumulate power. It is obvious in journalism, religion, politics, and law, to name just a few professions. My recent experiences, however, invite examination of how those needs can affect ordinary people in ordinary situations.

Readers of the Hebrew and Christian Scriptures (Deuteronomy 32 or Romans 12) are invited to leave vengeance to God, and be themselves more concerned about the kind of justice that puts things right for all. The work of the Truth and Justice Commission in the new South Africa is probably the best modern attempt to enact these principles: white people's owning of what occurred under apartheid sets everyone free. The need for revenge evaporates.

In my comic-book-reading days I used to fantasize about belonging to the Justice League of America, those superheroes who specialized in giving bad guys what they deserve. My recent experiences and my reflections on the French proverb have led to my resignation from the league. I will try to focus on putting things right rather than exposing things wrong. I'm hoping to be duller but more effective—and perhaps to smell better.

# CHAPTER TWO
## Not Far from the Kingdom

### The Spirituality of *The Sopranos*

One thing I heard most consistently while traveling in the United States, the United Kingdom, and Canada this summer was complaints about how *The Sopranos* ended, or failed to end.

It isn't easy for a writer of religious columns to bring up *The Sopranos*. The program is certainly a verbal and visual assault on what most of us consider decent, or even necessary, in storytelling. I wouldn't recommend it to my children or my parents. Persons of Italian descent were in some cases offended that once again organized crime is portrayed as an Italian project.

At the same time, the program captured the imaginations of many Americans for the best part of a decade. Why? You can get gratuitous sex and bad language every night on Cinemax. There had to be something else that drew people to HBO's *The Sopranos* and got everybody from Dick Cavett to America's leading psychiatric professors to write about it.

Perhaps for most viewers the attraction was the invitation to identify with the complexity of the characters, the familiar interplay of personal and family issues, and the recognition of the attempt most of us make at one time or another to do one thing and try to teach our children to do another. Tony's attempt to inhabit two worlds does not work for him, and so begins his journey with Dr. Melfi.

Without giving anything away to those who don't know the details, what I heard over the summer in three countries was the consistent complaint that after seven years, the series ends without much being resolved. Lots of people are dead, but the issues are all still alive, and danger lurks everywhere. None of Tony's problems are resolved.

To our unease at the unresolved nonending, I suggest: *that's the way life really is.* We are conditioned by the entertainment world to expect issues to be resolved, often with a happy ending, in two hours or less. Like Tony, we live with the fantasy that there is a magical fix to our problems, that we can go back to the security of childhood. In one episode he counters his daughter's desire to be a woman of her times by claiming that in his house "it is still 1954."

*The Sopranos* isn't going to teach anybody religion, but spiritual truths emerge quite clearly from time to time. The first lesson has to do with humility and patience: life is complex and cannot be reduced to a set of black-and-white definitions, and most of us will die with many unresolved issues and our children will continue to struggle with them.

The second has to do with integrity. Absent psychopathology ("vertical splitting"), we cannot easily contain within ourselves wildly contradictory thoughts, actions, and values. Tony's attempts to do so are part of what makes him a psychiatric patient. Nobody in the series works hard to have the purity of heart that wills only one thing, and the results mirror what we see each day in a less entertaining way.

The third has to do with charity and boundaries. Because life is complex and everybody's acts are determined by multiple motives and impulses, almost all of our judgments about other people's souls must be held in abeyance, even though we can and must have boundaries about their behavior.

It is equally mistaken to try to focus on "the good" in Tony or simply to condemn him. Both must be acknowledged. Tony is *Everyone* writ very large, wanting to do the right thing but carrying the obstacles within him.

To dwell on these topics is to ask the right questions. It is part of what the ancient writers called "preparation for the good news." To have the questions put so strongly in the guise of powerful entertainment may not be a bad thing at all.

## In the Water with Us

It was my first experience of sickening terror. I remember the gray sky, the chilly breeze, and my helplessness. Elizabeth was in danger of drowning. We kids at the church youth event were terrified. It was the late 1950s and today's strict standards for supervision were not in place and the nearest grown-up was out of earshot.

I knew I should just get in the water and help her, but was paralyzed by stories I'd heard at home of people who drowned while trying to save others. None of us were strong swimmers. In our impotence to help, we shouted: "Kick . . . you can make it . . . swim!"

An older kid who was coming to get his boat saw what was happening. He didn't shout advice. He didn't say anything. He got into the water and towed Elizabeth to the little dock from which we had been diving. She had been only twenty feet from us.

We could have given her good advice right up to the moment she drowned. The person who made the difference was the one who silently got into the water with her.

There are times in life that call for wisdom. There are those moments, however, when we need somebody in the water with us if the situation is to change. A few weeks after that incident, I left for boarding school. I never saw Elizabeth again, except at the other side of church at holidays. I hadn't the nerve or the vocabulary to ask her how it felt to be alone in the water, or what it felt like when the young man joined her.

I do know, however, what it feels like to stand alone at terrible places in life, places where advice is pointless and companionship is everything.

Muslims, Jews, and Christians revere the words of Isaiah, who spoke to a frightened king of humanity's need for something beyond words by naming a child Immanuel—"God is with us." Christians see that theme played to its fullest crescendo in the birth of Jesus the Messiah, "God with us" for all humanity. The idea of a divine figure experiencing human birth without a human father is not unknown in world religions—but something is different here. In telling the story of Bethlehem, the virgin, the star, and the magi, Christians try to make two points.

The first is that, although God had given advice in many and various ways through prophets, when the point was to be made for all time, God got into the water with us in the birth of a fragile and vulnerable human baby, who lived our life and died our death and has gone to the fullness of new life ahead of us. There is no part of human experience, from its joys to its horrors, from which God wishes to remain aloof.

The second point is that, when they insist that the Christ was a real human being, Christians see the affirmation of human worth. That the Creator would take up the reality of the creature expresses a dignity in human life that is absolute. When they take their own rhetoric seriously, Christians see each life as sacred. Whenever the Christian religion has been used to justify harm or neglect, it has been defiled. When it is employed to help people experience their worth in God's sight, the music is being played well.

In the months between Christmas, Good Friday, and Easter, there is time to observe what that child grew up to do and say. In December it is enough to remember my drowning friend and recall that, in a world full of advice givers, God still wants to be in the water with each of us. Merry Christmas!

## Looking at Life's Signals

There are, indeed, atheists in foxholes. War has made cynics of many. The ability of a species to kill and maim its own kind makes it difficult for some people to see a kind Creator behind our life.

I know firsthand stories of others, however, for whom war was the gateway to belief. One was George, a combat infantryman in Italy, a member of a platoon of New Englanders who prided themselves on their foul language, abusive behavior, and other crude acts of macho self-assurance normal in times of stress and fear.

George and his buddies were outraged when, after sustaining some losses in combat, their Yankee outfit received from the replacement depot a Texan who brought a Bible with him. They were waiting to heap abuse on him if he spouted religion, but he did not say a word. Still, they were upset by his presence. They did everything they could to get him to surrender his quiet manner.

When they went into battle, George and his buddies were as terrified as one might appropriately be in a situation where people are trying to kill each other. Their anxiety came out in the usual brutish ways. Their newcomer, however, remained calm even when things were at their worst.

My friend George said he could no longer deny that this stranger had something he did not have. For selfish reasons alone he had to "look into this God business." The rest has been a sixty-year adventure of faith.

Since hearing that story I have been looking for a parallel in my experience.

It occurred to me that there is also a person in my life who is immersed in the peace that God gives. By any standard he is among the most intelligent, charming, and wise people on the planet, and produces uniformly excellent work. He is also utterly without ambition. He has rejected numerous invitations to the top and still accomplishes a great deal.

After I had known and admired him for several years I got in his face a bit about this. I asked him very directly why, when he is a natural for positions most of us could not even imagine occupying, he has not seized his opportunities and become the genuinely great personage he could easily be, with all the rights and benefits that come with that status. I have been chewing on his answer for months.

He said quietly, "I discovered how much influence a person can have when they don't care who gets the credit."

It takes a great deal of personal security to make that statement. It takes enormous commitment to the betterment of human life to say it. It totally redefines success. More than that, it illustrates to me what human beings can be and do when they are willing to live into the fullness of peace.

This is why I remain a believer. Jesus promised his followers peace, adding quickly that he did not mean peace in the ordinary sense of cessation of hostility, but the kind of peace that comes from knowing that one's life is entirely secure in the worst of circumstances. That is not a matter of positive thinking, but of a living relationship of trust that the God who raised Christ will see us through any of the challenges of life or death.

There is only one way to find out if this is true, of course, and that is, as my friend in Italy put it, to look into it. Who gives you that signal in your life?

---

## God and the Solitary Golfer

Actually, I *can* worship God while playing golf—no matter what preachers say. The experience of the swing, when it is right, with body and mind working together as all the muscles remember their part of the dance, is about as holistic an experience as most of us are likely to get this side of hang gliding or figure skating. The experience of the "ping" when body, club, and ball connect right is a moment out of time, always new. I remember the biblical words "Behold, I am fearfully and wonderfully made."

When I allow myself to play golf without feelings of competition or performance anxiety, I reconnect with myself. In the truly restorative beauty of the world of green things, I meet the Creator.

I like being alone on the course. I used to play golf in the late weekday afternoons, when courses are least full. My favorite was laid out on Long Island's Great South Bay. That one can feel both energy and peace at the same time was its principal revelation to me, as the ghosts of the great whaling ships could be faintly detected on the gray waves.

Chances are that if my calling in life had not been to ordained ministry, reflecting on nature and its God would be the total of my religion. By natural inclination I would be among those who insist they can worship God on the golf course as well as they can anywhere else. In a limited sense, that claim would be true.

It is precisely because I can get what I think are my spiritual needs met by a walk and the experience of mind/body unity, however, that the weekly discipline of the liturgy is so important to my salvation. The liturgy essentially says to me, "You may have the other six days and twenty-two hours for solitary contemplation; there is nothing wrong with that; but for now you will pray with other disciples of Jesus."

Gathered into the church I find myself gathered into the most amazing company. Many are people whom I would not normally seek out; many would not normally seek me out. But here we are—astonishingly made kin to one another by our single faith and our one baptism. Their burdens become mine as we pray for all sorts and conditions of humanity.

Our mission and how God has equipped us for it are made real to me as the Bible is read and preached. As we enter the heart of our faith by sharing Christ's meal, I rediscover a wider world.

That world still has contemplation, golf, and music in it, to be sure, but it has people and issues. They call for words and acts of compassion, justice, and reconciliation. It has slums, and office towers, and bedroom communities in which the beauty of the flowers and our connectedness to the Creator and creation need desperately to be known. Self-interest is in this discipline, too: I have never dragged myself to church during vacation time without gaining a heightened sense of connection to the gifts of God that can be received only in sharing life with others.

After some years away with a shoulder injury, I will be back out there this summer during vacation. I can almost taste how good that will be, how refreshing, how cleansing, and I will thank and praise God for it all and during it all. I will also allow myself to be kept in touch with the even deeper realities of life in Christ. With these two aspects of life working together, I expect re-creation for sure.

---

## Beating the Inner Reptile

Biologists tell us that the lowest part of our brain has a simple method of sorting perceptions: Same—good. Different—kill or run away. In this "reptilian brain" that we share with all vertebrates lies the root of racism, sexism, classism, snobbery, and sectarianism.

The spiritual or moral history of our species could be written as a struggle not to kill or run away from what is different—how we learn to treat those with whom we cannot identify.

"Remember that you were strangers once," Moses reminded Israel. Writing to the Christians of Ephesus, St. Paul begs that we lead a life worthy of our calling, "with all lowliness and meekness, with patience, forbearing one another in love, eager to maintain the unity of the Spirit in the bond of peace." The apostle is up against nature, and he knows it. He asks us not to assume that anybody else has motives worse than our own. It is especially important to be "lowly and meek" when we are sure that we are right. This is true in part because there are other people in the room who know they are right, too.

Forbearing one another in love is a religious way of saying that because we value one another we don't crush one another. How does one do that? An experiment comes to mind. Focus on the noisiest, most headstrong person in the room (excepting yourself) and just love them. Love the frightened person inside them who feels they must fight to survive. Love the ignorant person inside them who doesn't know any better than to bully or terrorize. Love the trapped person inside them who has formed such bad habits that they don't even know they are objectionable. Love the parts of them that most remind you of what you fear in yourself.

It is humbling but helpful to realize that we exist because others have been practicing just this experiment. The ancient story says that we are here because God didn't crush Adam and Eve. Individually we know that we are here because our parents and loved ones didn't throw us out when we were being, well, unattractive. If you really doubt that others ever had to just put up with your wackiness, and did it because they loved you, ask around. Start with those who love you most.

Paul wants us "eager" to maintain the bond of peace. That eagerness is the least reptilian value imaginable, and in Paul's mind it is the gift of the Holy Spirit. That is one of the reasons Jesus told his disciples to share his body and blood: you can't easily eat with people you reject. It is the spiritual gift that can work with our wonderfully complex brains and inspire creative ways to love, to overcome dissension.

An even bigger gift of the Spirit is to come to difficult discussions eager to help people work things out, to find a way. Such eagerness, for me, is religion at its best. In that eagerness the Spirit nourishes and sustains the community of the Church.

The Church is a society into which I am called by Christ. I tear or destabilize it at great peril to my soul. Every existing division is the result of human sin. We just divert attention by arguing about whose.

Have you ever noticed that the story about sin entering the world is about a snake? We are rightly scared of snakes' fangs and their ability to crush. The message from St. Paul is much stronger: Don't hate them for their bodies—hate them for their brains, and thrive in the community of the Spirit.

## What Do They Eat?

When Diana and I made thirteen presentations around our fourteen-county Diocese of Bethlehem about our visit to our partnership Diocese of Kajo Keji, a frequent question about our Sudanese sisters and brothers was: "What do they eat?"

After I quipped that there was no McDonald's in Kajo Keji, we stressed that they ate radically different and the same food, with sincere and joyful hospitality.

Let me explain.

If you are not at my son's favorite restaurant by six on the night of the Brooklyn bakery run, the cannoli are gone. To people from the old neighborhood, there's only one kind of cannoli. Each cannoli is treated as precious.

Thirty years after my grandmother's death, the only authentic *kruschiki* are those my sister makes once a year from grandma's recipe. On the other side, only my mother (and now Diana) makes a certain kind of German apple cake.

When I shared my quest for perfect Kaiser rolls and rye bread on our diocesan Internet list, e-mail came from many who don't live where they were born.

There's more than one way to feel away from home. We yearn for God, sensing the distance. We sense our distance from those who have gone before us and from the Lord we wish to see more clearly. We grieve emotional distance from others. We feel at times like "a motherless child, a long way from home."

When we wayfaring pilgrims feel disconnected, lonely, yearning, or just generally "a long way from home," the Body and Blood of Christ are a precious taste of food from home.

Eating *kruschiki* reconnects me instantly with a large part of my experience, including a tough little woman's journey from Bremerhaven to a new life in a new country.

Eucharist reconnects me instantly with the meaning of my life, with the carpenter whose journey through death to new life gives me life, with those in the room and with all who have been to Christ's table at all times and in all places.

Almost the first thing out of my grandmother's mouth, when I visited, was the affectionate command: "Eat." I didn't know then that sharing food is how people establish, renew, and solidify relationships. Eating together is not a casual thing.

Think of Jesus' wisdom in commanding his disciples to have at the center of their practices a simple meal. In Luke's Gospel account, the Last Supper takes place in the middle of a fight among the disciples!

I can easily recall that the Body and Blood of my Lord are really present at the altar. Sometimes I need God's help to remember that this really is a meal. God has put us at table together so the daily disagreements, the impatience, the frustrations, and the challenges of living together may be transcended.

In medicine, science, and religion all great new truths begin as blasphemies of a sort. Imagine the look on the disciples' faces when Jesus took that cup and said, "This is my blood, for you." To those who thought he had gone too far, he encouraged openness to the menu: Go ahead. Take it. Eat it. Drink it.

To us who would like to remain a bit disconnected from or incurious about each other, Eucharist is an adventure. Surprise looms. We don't know whom we will be next to, with whom Christ is reconnecting us.

We experience the Body of Christ in the sacrament within that everelastic and exciting context of the Body of Christ that is the Church. Motherless children, people far from home, folks feeling like outsiders, people who need to escape being insiders: *Eat.*

## On the Money: The Practical Atheist

One of the most challenging pieces of theological literature I have ever read is on the dollar bill: "In God we trust." Whether those words belong there is for judges to decide. In either event, the slogan stands in pointed contrast to the attitudes of most Christians and Jews I know. Most people I know are atheists. I suspect they would be offended to hear me say so.

Most Americans believe that God exists, but most of us lead our lives as though there were no God, and no basic commitments that govern ordinary living. We would have to admit that what we know of God was not on our mind the last time we spoke impatiently or rudely to a loved one, the last time we slightly adjusted the numbers on our tax returns, or the last time we allowed ourselves the luxury of speaking of some person or group with contempt.

Real atheism is not just a question of belief. It is a question of actions that deny a basic relationship with God. It is one thing to say that God exists; but do we trust God and act on the basis of that relationship? In this sense, the most profound religious statement available to us on a daily basis is on the money we use.

Early Christianity concluded from the Scriptures and their experience of God that the one God was at the same time three persons. That boggles the mind. It's supposed to. Human language simply cannot contain the infinite. What each of us can understand is that when speaking this way of God, Christians are at the very least saying that God is essentially and eternally in relationship, in communion, in love.

When the New Testament says that God is love, it is not a throwaway line or a sentimentality; it is a tough-minded conclusion about what is the highest and greatest value. To believe in God in the sense that our money puts it when it says, "In God we trust," is to take the risk of living that trust by loving where and when it is not convenient to love.

I have seen this recently in my primary care physician. She has begun to treat some patients on public assistance at no charge because they would otherwise have to wait for six weeks for a clinic appointment to treat what could kill them in three weeks. She is bucking the ethos of her profession, which continues to hold that health care is a privilege, and bucking the societal idea that the poor should only have table scraps. She is bucking the system because her faith tells her that compassion is more important than comfort.

People tend to think in magical terms about God. When human evil causes a great tragedy, the cry goes up, "How could God have let this happen?" as though it is somehow God's job to underwrite human efforts and neutralize every act of human will except our own. Trusting God would move us from magical thinking to, uncomfortable as it is to say, obedience.

The dollar bill can remind us to take very seriously the cumulative effect of human evil, evil of both the everyday and catastrophic types.

Until we see our own brokenness and arrogance, talk of God is meaningless, merely veneer. To get past our practical atheism is to undertake the hard work of monitoring our actions and motives at precisely those times when it is inconvenient to do so. That would amount to taking money seriously at last.

## Finding God

Sometimes we have trouble finding God for the same reason a thief has trouble finding a police officer. We know that to live in a relationship with God would change things. We fear that something we don't want to give up would have to go. We fear we would have to enter a relationship we could not control and a world we could not predict, an untidy world. Worst of all, we would have to wrestle with the notion that some force or personality allows the worst of what we do to one another to happen. That does seem to add cosmic insult to daily injury.

Similarly, there is more than we want to hear in the story of Jesus' death and resurrection. Friends let him down; one friend even betrays him. Designated good people find it convenient to allow injustice. Women who know what is really going on are powerless to do anything about it. Government is far worse than useless.

Looked at this way, there is nothing extraordinary about this story. Routine bureaucratic evil in the world dehumanizes the poor. Unremarkable callousness makes cynics of us all. Evil's greatest triumph is to be so taken for granted that it goes unnoticed. Researchers have pointed to the dull, impersonal, machinelike efficiency of the Nazi holocaust as possibly its most revolting feature.

At our worst, we can perpetrate injustice and unaccountably comfort ourselves with the words, "It's nothing personal," when that is precisely the problem.

In the suffering and death of Jesus God asks us to see at least two things. In all of this happening to an innocent man, we are asked to see our habitual patterns of evil and violence exposed for what they are and to resolve never again to be part of them. But beyond that, we are invited to see in Jesus God's love remaining faithful to us despite the very worst we can do. "Father, forgive them" are words spoken out of just that love.

To proclaim the resurrection does not erase costly, messy, faithful love. It vindicates it. I recently read a book by an Israeli scholar who does not believe Jesus was the Messiah, but who believes God raised him. He claims there is no other explanation for so many lives changed, for the commitment and self-sacrifice of Christianity's first leaders.

The resurrection addresses the part of me that can't find God for the same reason that a thief cannot find a police officer. To open myself to relationship with God will change my life, take me to strange places, reorder my priorities, just as I fear. I will be asked to put compassion before convenience, purpose before pleasure, faithfulness before feelings, living before having—every bit of it a heresy against the creed my generation cherishes. To have anything to do with God will demand many small moments of agony, perhaps large ones.

Those who dare to live that way know something else, too. Moments that may feel like death are nothing compared with the exhilaration—or the quiet joy—of new life that follows. The feeling of strength that comes from discovering integrity. The joy of seeing love replace wrath. The sunshine and flowers that can be seen when we learn to look beyond ourselves.

Christians believe that Christ's resurrection is the promise of life with God forever. We sometimes forget, however, that forever includes today. When we dare to live with God and for others, the power of the resurrection is ours.

There is only one way to discover if this is true, and that is to try it.

## Religion Gave Him the Wrong God

As I write, I am looking at a wind-driven soybean field in Ohio, steeling myself for a memorial service for an in-law of whom I was very fond.

There will be recountings of happy memories, Beatles music with a video presentation of photos, other pieces of 1960s nostalgia, and a party-style luncheon with a NASCAR theme. The truth about Jerry will never be told, because religion is being carefully locked out.

For most of his life, Jerry never encountered religion that wasn't demanding, condemning, black-and-white. The religion he encountered had no room for his own challenges, unhappiness, and life pain. He learned to think of religion, of God himself, as enemy.

He tried to do his duty, providing for his family; he tried to enjoy some of the pleasures of life. At fifty-nine, he had a ponytail second only to Willy Nelson's in vintage and color. His key cultural icon was James Dean.

He attended the annual memorial services, rode his Hogs, and shared in the Dean who in real life and on film just couldn't connect. To use the word of those days, he was alienated without fully knowing why.

He rejected Christian fundamentalism, but had nothing to put in its place; so he pulled back from religion entirely. More than once he said, "But what if they're right?" If he didn't accept the package, would he toast in hell forever? Like many who had been traumatized by or through religion, he couldn't really process a middle ground. He retained fear instilled at an early age and that nagging fear fueled resentment.

In the last ten years of his life, however, he began to find a different way. Some of the chemical buffers he had put between himself and his pain went away. He began to deal with reality face-to-face. He worked on being a father. He made some difficult choices and entered a companionship that gave him a chance to relearn a lot about relationship and its transforming power. He didn't live long enough in a new world of relating, loving, and reflecting for the religious questions to transform with the rest of him.

There are those who love him dearly but who still mourn him as a lost soul cooking in hell. I am not so ready to do that. Jerry travailed and was heavy laden. It was to such as he that Jesus offered rest and refreshment.

Jerry was not without a spiritual side, but he was never evangelized in words he could hear, in concepts with which he could identify, in a way that truly set him free from the idea of religion as escape from punishment. I see him as a seeker who was ready for more transformation, but who didn't live long enough for it to manifest itself very much in language.

He took an interest in my work and would discuss these very newspaper columns but he had not yet fully come to the place where he sensed the Son of Man would be seen eating with him as he did with Zaccheus and so many others. He didn't yet realize that God was for him.

Knowing where he was in his journey, I have no trouble committing him to the care of God in whose knowledge, vision, and service he will grow. The prayer I have for him is one that includes the words, "may his heart and soul now ring out in joy to you." It's what he was searching for all his life. It's what religion made it hard for him to find. It's what his new relationships were pointing him to.

The Christ who said, "I have not come to condemn the world"—the secret Christ for some of us—give his soul the peace that religion denied it.

## Faith Is What You Die For; Dogma Is What You Kill For

I have a friend who is paralyzed because of the carelessness of religious leaders. He walks and talks perfectly, but freezes up completely when he faces issues of faith or morality.

He grew up in a time when religious leaders reacted to the explosion of new ideas and freedoms in the culture by tightening restrictions. The only way my friend could live in the last quarter of the twentieth century was to reject entirely religious thinking that was too organized or that tried to set rigid standards for moral behavior.

Trying to make decisions on questions of faith or morality floods him with painful memories. Because he does not want to hurt others as he was hurt, he draw boundaries. His frustration over this is poorly disguised. I see his anguish even as he makes claims to being "open" or "nonjudgmental."

Actually, I have many friends like this man. Their suffering is real. They are deep and careful thinkers so frightened of reproducing the repressive religion of their youth that their own children have appeared on the scene as young adults largely undeveloped morally and spiritually. We read daily about the suffering this produces.

There has been a good side to this paralysis. People like my friend keep the doors open in many expressions of Judaism and Christianity to new thinking and to the very old thinking of other spiritual traditions. We have a better idea of what is generally religious and what the distinctive insights of our own faith traditions may be. Religious leaders have gotten better at listening, have had their perspectives broadened, and have been able to learn as well from people whose experience would have been completely ignored by another generation.

For the sake of those who have grown up with little or no moorings, it is time to gather what we have learned from many voices and teach religion in a way that people who are not religious studies majors can put to work in their lives.

How do we do this without creating a new rigidity? One safeguard is suggested by an observation about the history of all religions that has been haunting me: Faith is what you would die for; dogma is what you would kill for. Certainly, an exaggeration—but there's enough truth in it to lie heavily on my mind.

Religious persons need to get better at stating in the language of testimony and invitation what they would die for. Moral and spiritual teachings that are based on faith's deepest convictions sound quite different from those that arise out of a need to punish what one fears.

In both cases one might say "Thou shalt not kill," but the commandment sounds different when it comes from reverence for life and its Creator. I firmly believe that Christians are bound to the teachings of the Scriptures, but I want to say that in a way that reflects my faith, not my anger or fear.

Fear asks, "What ideas would we kill for?"—another way of saying, "What ideas make us truly afraid?" When religious (and secular) communities and institutions dare to ask that question honestly, their response to what brings the fear can be more reasoned and compassionate than those overreactions that have created generations of paralyzed believers.

This is not to say that wrong will become right, but that moral principles based on the need to kill what one fears are far less helpful (or convincing) than those that go beyond the fears to speak of what we trust and rejoice in.

## Learning from What Jesus Did Not Do

No doubt the best-known verse of the New Testament is John 3:16, "For God so loved the world that he gave his only Son, so that everyone who believes in him may not perish but may have eternal life." We may not know the next verse so well. "Indeed, God did not send the Son into the world to condemn the world, but in order that the world might be saved through him."

Sometimes, an exercise in discovering who Jesus is *not* and what he did *not* do helps us focus on who he is and what he is about.

Jesus did *not* give in to the disciples' desire to have more power than others. Jesus did *not* stop healing people on the Sabbath, even when he was told to cut it out. Jesus did *not* force anyone to believe in him. Jesus did *not* stay away from people who were blind, deaf, mute, diseased, possessed by an evil spirit, paralyzed, or rejected by others.

Most of all, Jesus did *not* condemn those who were pushed to the edges of life. He ate and associated with those who had received no other message from society but that they were outcasts—hateful to God, hateful to humanity. To them, he said that whatever real sins they had were forgiven. To them, for whom the hardest thing to believe was that God thought they were worth paying attention to, he brought healing and wholeness and salvation. Jesus' mere announcement that he planned to visit the home of one robber baron named Zaccheus stimulated immediate change.

The ministry of "not condemning" was one of the most radical things Jesus did. For that, he was condemned, because he was tearing down the carefully drawn boundaries that assured the people in the middle and the top of their superiority. Lest we in turn feel immensely superior to that ancient culture, it might be worth asking how good our own culture is at not condemning. I read recently that two-thirds of gay and lesbian students are threatened or attacked each year in school, that high school students hear antigay language twenty-six times each school day, and that teachers who witness antigay behavior do nothing about it almost all of the time. Teachers' silence allows condemnation to stand, and we all know the very high rate of suicide among gay teens.

What has been your experience? How easy is it in school, in the workplace, and in social settings to find a willing ear for ridicule or condemnation? "Who sinned, this man or his parents, that he was born blind?" Jesus' disciples once asked him and discovered that he threw their question entirely out of court. Demonic voices today say people have AIDS because they have sinned. "It's your fault." This is said and heard by Christians.

Condemning does reinforce our sense of order and control. I suppose it is easier to condemn victims of plague or poverty than to stare into the abyss of pointless suffering. But that harder job does seem to be ours. The immediate response to suffering is to be compassionate, but for those who wish to grow spiritually there is a bit more work to do, and that means acknowledging our own need for healing.

It is the part of us that nervously asks whose fault it is that people are sick that needs healing. It takes courage, but our acknowledgment that assigning blame gives us a sense of security and innocence is the beginning of that healing. Reading John 3:16 and 17 back-to-back until we see how they belong together in our lives can put that healing in motion.

## What Makes Grace Amazing

I can still see the veins bulging in his neck. I had suggested a break in our strenuous conversation because I was afraid of his anger and that he might have a stroke on the spot. I also knew I wasn't getting through. Convulsed with rage, he shouted across a very small room, "I am *not* angry." The door slammed as he stormed out into the Minneapolis winter thirty-four years ago.

It was a long time before I saw Bill again. When we did reconnect I tried out some advice I had been given by an older and wiser colleague to whom I had told the story. He suggested that the man didn't need me to correct his thinking, to help him identify his feelings, or to get through to him at all. He suggested that Bill needed me to be patient with him as he raved because Bill was more afraid of his anger than I was.

So I sat there. As he denounced the societal changes of the 1970s, Bill used every racial slur I had heard and some that were new to me. It took two hours, but the storm passed. We were suddenly something like friends, and got on well for the couple of years left in his life.

My insightful advisor knew what is at the heart of the biblical tradition: God can stand us. If God can stand us, we may be able to stand ourselves. The most important thing we can communicate to others is not that God loves them *in spite of* what they are doing, but that God loves them while they are doing it.

Here's the problem: we don't usually love them when they are like that. Yet, it remains true that most people can change only when they believe they are safe.

The price we pay for civilization—for evolution itself—is that we live in a constant tension. On the one hand, there are peace, productivity, and harmony. On the other, our destructive tendencies. So that we, our families, and our communities may thrive, we rein in some of our impulses. Reining them in is one thing. Pretending they don't exist is quite another. Bill was afraid of his own rage and kept denying its existence even as it consumed him. Change was possible only when he experienced somebody else standing it and standing him.

My colleague was very wise indeed. The truth is that I need to be reminded of that story an awful lot. The biblical celebration that "while we were yet sinners" God loved us is in constant need of reinforcement. In October some of our neighbors celebrate the Protestant Reformation. Its insistence on God's grace is a reclaiming of the most basic truth of faith: God is for us.

The Christian message is that Jesus is the determinative expression of that truth. God being for us means that it is safe to be, to change, and to grow. None of that can happen until we allow ourselves to be grasped, however tentatively, by the truth that we are accepted by God precisely at our worst.

Dropping pretense and defense, excuse and rationalization, and letting that acceptance happen and bring change is where the religious code words "repentance" and "faith" begin to have their meaning. The absolute letting go of self-justification and denial is a hard truth to internalize—it is, as my geek friends say, counterintuitive.

It can happen when we discover that God can stand us. Then, truth goes to work. Freedom follows, and even joy. It is what makes grace amazing, again and again.

---

## Stop Being So Humble

Randy is eight years old and well on his way to an emotionally troubled life. He is very bright and does exceptionally well in school and the many activities into which he has been propelled. His parents have high standards and goals for him, but have decided not to tell him that all tests of both his aptitude and his achievement mark him as a prodigy.

He knows he is different, but does not know why. The parents' reason for not telling him has nothing to do with Randy but comes out of their own fantasy world. His mom said, "I hate it when people brag about being the smartest person in the room" and does not want her son thinking he is smarter than his peers (or his parents). Her son will live in a kind of emotional agony because of her fear and insecurity, and paradoxically may end up bragging in order to soothe the uncertainty about himself that the family is installing in his mind.

Sad to say, the conversation got worse. There was a bit more parental bragging about the boy: in religious instruction classes his written list of things about himself that needed improvement was more than twice as long as his assessment of his gifts. For this he received praise. At a tender age he is encouraged to be overscrupulous while living with an uncertain sense of his place in the world.

Beyond my concern for a young man who is being destined for a lot of emotional pain, I find it very sad that yet again religion is being used to reinforce that pain. Christians often misread St. Paul's admonition that nobody should "think more highly of themselves than they ought" as meaning they ought not think highly of themselves. This misreading is odd because of all the characters in the Christian Scriptures, St. Paul most clearly had a high esteem for his own gifts—what he asks of us is realism about ours.

There is an alternative to the destructive and conflicted sense of humility being installed in Randy's thinking. It comes from a story about blind ambition to which Jesus gave new sight.

When two of the twelve disciples, James and John, were bursting for recognition and greatness to the irritation of their companions and demanded to be seated at his immediate left and right, Jesus did not squelch their ambition or advocate a false humility. He redirected ambition. "Whoever would be great among you, must be servant of all," was his response, adding that he himself came to serve rather than to be served. On these terms who dares not to be great?

Human ambition and drive can be conflicted, infantile, and power obsessed. That same ambition and drive can be directed toward accomplishments that contribute to the common good, and here Jesus baptizes ambition. There is nothing wrong with wanting to be the best; there is everything right with being the best when your best makes a contribution to the world.

I suggest that the word to Randy needs to be two-dimensional. The first is to let him celebrate the truth about himself so that he can rejoice in his gifts without being suspicious of them. If he is that good, he should exult in what he has been given. The second is to help him use his gifts to make a contribution to the world around him, an attitude that brings quiet and very deep joy that requires no bragging.

# CHAPTER THREE
## Bittersweet Love

**A** **FREQUENT THEME IN** the columns is human love. Part of that comes from my sadness at the suffering that repeatedly occurs in American families. In my own life, of our circle of young couples married in 1969, only two marriages remain intact. As a parish priest I have been with those whose intimate relationships have become sources of pain—and those who simply quit when relationships offered challenges. Consequently, I often try to emphasize to a consumer culture that love is an investment, and tend to underscore its costs and responsibilities as much as its joy. There is reference to pain here, and the reader will sense my life-long fascination with St. Paul's mysticism of the cross lurking not far beneath the surface. The constant crossing from human love to divine love and back again gives the spiritual life its rhythm and its resilience. These pieces were written at an average interval of about two years, providing opportunity to repeat the themes of giving, acceptance, and joy along with fairly constant reference to Archbishop Thomas Cranmer's ingenious phrase "With my body I thee worship."

## Irreconcilable Differences

Someone recently mentioned friends who decided to divorce less than a year into their marriage. He wondered aloud if he may have put more effort into his friendship with them than they put into their marriage. He was not a person who judges others. He was frustrated at how quickly his friends justified their decision by an appeal to irreconcilable differences.

In many jurisdictions in this country, divorces may be obtained on the grounds of irreconcilable differences. I suppose this is the legal justification for so-called "no-fault" divorce, i.e., one that does not require one party, often with painful contention, to blame the other for the breakdown of the marriage. I have wondered, however, how many "no-fault" divorces may be the result of "no-effort" marriages.

My experience is that successful marriages have several, even many, irreconcilable differences. Husbands and wives learn, despite their differences, to be reconciled with one another. Their love for and commitment to each other enable them to live with and love through their differences, even to be playful about how each relates with the other through such difference.

Sometimes those differences are in time even resolved. Relationship requires patience with the complexity of the other. All of this, of course, requires some minimum of life experience and maturity.

St. Paul urges Christians to be reconciled to God and one another because in the mystery of reconciliation we discover our true union with Christ. The practice of reconciliation among people leads to and from the truth of our reconciliation with God. It is good to read chapter five of Paul's Second Letter to the Corinthians and chapter two of his Letter to the Ephesians.

Reconciliation is not about finding out who is right, although sometimes that must also happen. It is not about the exercise of power that we call forgiveness, although that often must happen. Reconciliation with God is not a juridical process. It begins with accepting the fact that we are accepted and embraced by God on a level far beyond score keeping about behavior.

Reconciliation among Christians is about encountering others in the way that God sees and values them, in the embrace he opened to us on the cross. As we attempt to follow Jesus, we journey toward the center of this experience; still, we know how even a little fear can cast out love. We know what St. Paul means we he writes of a "dividing wall of hostility," though we might think here of a dividing wall of complexity.

Think about your friends and perhaps yourself. You may find successful marriages where introverts love extroverts, where extroverts love introverts, where someone who scans his universe with his head loves someone who scans her universe with her heart, and vice versa. They love and have learned to live with each other's complexity.

It may not always be possible to reconcile what some consider irreconcilable differences. There is, however, the reality of patience with and understanding of one another's complexity.

When we approach one another out of strength, indignation, or the old standby of hurt feelings, some things might be resolved and some goals might be met, but the gospel will not be experienced and the walls will stay up.

When we come to each other undefended and vulnerable as God's children alive by Christ's grace, only then can newness of life come forth.

You may find this difficult. I do. It requires work and the discipline of prayer to overcome our more primitive responses and encounter one another as God relates with us. The fruits, however, have no parallel in human experience.

## New Year's Resolutions for Lovers

No pet lover would feed a pet a steady diet of table scraps. It would weaken health, shorten life, and possibly kill by choking. How many of us, though, nurture our closest relationships with leftovers?

I have become aware that many marriages run on scraps. They end badly; or perhaps worse, they just grind on. This is the scenario: both partners get out of bed with a list of things to do already churning in their brains. They work hard and do a creditable job all day at home or the job. Then they do useful things at home or in the community in the evening hours. Finally they plop back into bed too tired even for meaningful conversation, perhaps being briefly present to one's spouse in some halfhearted way. And they wonder where the pizzazz went.

Television psychologist Dr. Phil says that loss of libido among married people has reached epidemic proportion. I do not know if that is true, but my encounters with people suggest that his observation covers only a symptom. The larger problem, loss of relationship, has reached pandemic proportion.

People do not seem to be budgeting their emotional energy nearly so wisely as they are investing their retirement funds. Two people running at a high level of energy all day find that their greatest need at the end of the day is rest—they have squandered the resources required to love, honor, and cherish. They have been too busy with good things to have time or energy for the best things.

There may be reasons for that. Even the richest people stay busy to avoid feeling their emotional poverty. If prodded, they may defensively say that their spouse's need for relationship is unreasonable considering all they have to do. Here we see that unfaithfulness to vows takes many forms. Not being emotionally present is one of them.

January is the secular season of repentance, a word that simply means turning around from the overeating and overspending of the December holidays. Three resolutions may add a bit of nourishment for relationship in place of scraps.

First, nourish your spirit. You cannot give what you do not have. Self-care is a duty if you are going to be a lover. Many people find it helpful to have some period each day, perhaps only ten minutes, when they do nothing. They sit still, eyes unfocused or closed, and do not think. Going to a quiet place inside takes learning for some, for others it is as easy as listening to their own breathing. It is a fundamental act of self-care that recharges and repairs the soul. Do not do this while driving. For others, listening to music is a cleansing and restoring moment. The point is that, just as surely as one takes vitamins each day, it is useful to take time to nourish the spirit.

The second resolution is trickier. Do slightly less: trim enough from the daily list so there is something to give at home. Obviously, most tasks and opportunities will still be there tomorrow—what is surprising is they won't seem so urgent. To be faithful to one's vows requires a deliberate conservation of energy.

Finally, enjoy each other. After the kids are in bed, do something together for half an hour, with the TV off. Some couples read a book together, others discuss the newspaper, some play a game or have a joint hobby. Others just enjoy talking. The truest of lovers share their interior journeys.

Change is cumulative. A nation populated with people invested in care of self, conservation of energy, and intentional presence with their beloved might give Dr. Phil less to worry about.

## Desire and Forgiveness

I started to grow one day in 1967 when I had a fight with my girlfriend. She said and did something to me that hurt me to the core of my being. Then she did something worse. She apologized. There are times when to respond "no problem" to an apology is an obscenity. This would have been such a time.

My love for her and my desire for union with her made me want to forgive her. Then a curious frustration started. I soon realized that by forgiving her I gave up the right to look hurt, to appear the victim, to sulk, and to make her suffer by seeing my pain. I had not planned on losing that arsenal of subtle revenge. So *this* is what it is like to be an adult, I thought, with a touch of regret.

Old habits die hard. I rather automatically tried to sulk, but could not. The encounter was life-giving and slightly frustrating. The best I could manage was to look sort of convalescing, which is not very satisfying and slightly comic. Something died in me that day, at least a little. Its death was a release. Habitual recourse to outrage or victimhood simply perpetuates suffering and the habits themselves are quite aggressive. On the other hand, having the upper hand morally and using it to reconcile rather than punish gives life to all around.

I have written several times that our souls are in the most danger—and we are potentially the most dangerous to others—when we believe that we are in the right. No other statement in this space has gotten quite the same degree of angry correspondence from religious people. Many heard me suggesting that there is something wrong with being right or that there is no such thing as absolute truth or that there is no right and wrong. That is not the point. The point is that crusaders tend to kill.

"While we were yet sinners, God loved us," wrote St. Paul long ago. To forgive comes not from being satisfied that an offense is paid for, but from the desire to overcome separation and hostility. Jesus was at his most infuriating when his first word from the cross was, "Father, forgive them," even offering an excuse for his enemies, that they did not know what they were doing.

To forgive someone while they are still hurting you is to inhabit a level of compassion that most of us seldom visit, except perhaps with our children. The wound my girlfriend gave me hurt for a long time. Its scar still throbs and may do so forever, just as my arm would remain chopped off if that is what she had done to me. Forgiveness does not fix; but it can heal or, perhaps, overcome. Forgiving what still hurts is the gateway to freedom and maturity; it is a narrow gate, however, something like the eye of a needle.

In Holy Week, Christians observe the days of Christ's death and resurrection. When we see human nature—our nature, not that of some ancient individuals—at work in that act, we can recognize God's love overcoming sin as Christ continues to love us at our very worst. God desires us, thus St. John's telling of this story has the crucified Christ "drawing" people to him. John's picture is not so much that of a bill being paid, but the portrayal of love being faithful to my unloving self, a love that continually draws me to him and the way of life he offers.

## Love and Adventure

From a meeting in Canada, I concluded an e-mail to my wife, Diana, "I love you although and because that is an adventure." She is an understanding sort and got what I was struggling to say. Which is this: We seek a beloved who provides a secure base from which to explore life, someone with whom to share ecstasy, and an ally in the face of challenges. This is a gift not everyone receives. The adventure part begins when we realize that the beloved is not an "object," not even an "object of affection," but a real person outside of our control. Here is a person with will, agenda, and possibilities. To engage another truly and devotedly is not about freeze-drying a desirable set of characteristics with those deadly lyrics, "Don't go changing."

To love involves respecting what one contemplates, admires, and cherishes in the other, even as they change. An old ritual had it right: "With my body I thee worship." That sentiment is profoundly intimate; it also sets a boundary. We cannot truly worship and possess. Only idols do not change. To love others includes fostering their growth and applauding their increasing knowledge of who and what they are. Love includes binding their wounds as they struggle to work out their salvation. While this is challenge and adventure, it is also joy to see the beloved becoming someone more complete, more beautiful to behold.

Patiently making room for God's Spirit on a daily nonspectacular basis is one of the disciplines of loving until death do us part. It is not often comfortable but it is more often rewarding. I can only hope that my own evolution has brought Diana more joy than pain. She has certainly rolled with the punches. So it is both because and although loving is an adventure that I find that perseverance in its disciplines brings joy.

If what I have written is at all accurate about our most intimate relationships, I must ask what in the world St. Paul was thinking when he wrote to the Ephesians that the human spousal relation pointed to Christ and the Church. He uses the countercultural language of mutual submission, leaving space for the other to be, and honoring who and what they are. The posture of mutual submission is not one of demand or domination, but of service and flexibility.

Only this insight makes it possible for me to read Church history without walking away from Church or otherwise flinching; beyond the simple confession that Jesus is Lord, I can find nothing in Christianity that has not substantially evolved. Like any wise lover, in taking the Church to himself,

Christ took a spouse who would continually evolve, like any spouse. He must rejoice in that, as he abets it, having already said, "and you will do greater works than these."

Throughout the Christian tradition, both the individual soul and the Church are portrayed as spouse or even lover of Christ. This certainly is a great mystery and insists that the loving maintenance of relationship as parties grow and change over the years is at the core of any holy union. Should we not also expect that both God and the Church will continue to evolve? A God whom Scripture recalls saying, "Behold, I do a new thing," may offer change when I want permanence and peace, may offer bread when I want a stone. How like a lover!

People often get "hitched" (as the duchess of Cornwall put it) and come to religion looking for a sense of security and companionship. Much less commonly we come looking for adventure and change. We might as well welcome what is inevitable, for that is where the joy resides.

## Body Worship: Making Love

"Are you in love?" "No, we're just having sex." Sound familiar? The common expression, "having sex," is a clue to what our culture seems to miss about physical intimacy: the person, the giving, and the receiving. It also sounds mechanical, value free, and a bit boring. Where, in those two drab words, is passion, commitment, or ecstasy?

In my tradition the marriage rite originally said, "With my body I thee worship and with all my worldly goods I thee endow." *With my body I thee worship.* Making love takes on new possibilities when we see the pleasure we give as an act of worship—affirming the worth—of the other, moving as one flesh toward ecstasy.

This also means that casual, drunken, begrudging, unskilled, or predatory sexual acts are a kind of sacrilege, as are any acts that use, oppress, or humiliate another. That there have always been people who have eroticized just such moments is no more testimony to their appropriateness than the existence of tumors argues that cancer is a good thing because it occurs in nature. To eroticize or libidinize one's personal neediness is just as bad.

*With my body I thee worship.* It is not just the how of sex that needs to be taught. The what and the why that give humans the possibility for more sublime moments than doing what comes naturally can provide needs to be taught and taught again. *With my body I thee worship.* How did we lose those powerful words? The age in which the United States and my denomination first saw light was the Age of Reason. Along with its many advances, it brought a kind of sterility to the life of the body, emphasizing the life of the mind.

As people increasingly thought of their minds and bodies as separate departments, what the body did became less honorable. It was possible to separate the acts of mind and body completely. French philosopher Rousseau had nineteen illegitimate children by a number of women, put them all in orphanages, and then wrote a book about child rearing without feeling that anything might be wrong or even inconsistent with his doing so.

With heads divorced from the rest of their bodies, people reacted negatively to the phrase about body worship, because it so obviously meant what it said. And what it said was countercultural.

We never restored the phrase to the Episcopal marriage rite; nowadays it gets honorable mention, however, with its tasteful and altogether too tactful insertion of "with all that I am and all that I have, I honor you."

As language for worship, this is a failure, because it can float by us entirely unnoticed. It is a start, however, and is a great gift, because it makes the point that sex and money are indeed something we talk about, must talk about, in church. It is our entire lives that God wants to bless. It is our entire lives that we live in response to God's love.

We might want to rethink the erotic aspects of our lives from the point of view of spirituality. *Eros* does not necessarily mean "lust," but often means "desire for union." It is from this truth that so many Christian mystics—men and women—went on to see Christ as their lover; and the prophet Hosea described God as wooing back an unfaithful Israel. Learning to worship our own beloved means, first of all, honoring the desire we have for them as being from God.

In June we think of weddings; let's also think of the marriages. God has given us our own most intimate moments to allow us to communicate the worth of our spouse, and to make love indeed.

---

## A Grown-up Valentine

It's February, and soon the Valentine goodies will be given with smiles and received with blushes. Many women and not a few men, awaiting the one day in the year when their spouse will confess their deepest feelings for them, are already hoping they can make that single moment last for twelve months. Some will be profoundly disappointed when that does not happen, but right there we find the essence of real love. Starter love is infatuation, the idealization of the partner, and the denial of all that love costs. Consumerist love calls it off when love is costly or inconvenient.

But worthwhile love does cost. To love someone is to be vulnerable to them, and that vulnerability produces a fear or resentment that many people deny, preferring to live with the idealized image—until it crumbles. To love someone is to respect the fact that they will remain to some extent a mystery, ultimately unknowable, even after years. To love someone is to surrender the dream of controlling them, surrendering what are sometimes entirely legitimate expectations for the sake of the relationship. Finally, to love someone is to commit to a person with imperfections, some of which will cause deep and abiding pain; some people choose to live in denial of that reality and think that true love has left them behind.

The depth of love comes when we manage to embrace two truths. The beloved is indeed our prized person, occupying a special throne in our hearts. The beloved is also a source of vulnerability, pain, and therefore possible resentment. When we can keep all of these factors in healthy tension, we know the depth of love. It really isn't "for better *or* worse"; it's "for better *and* worse." When we can embrace the one who gives us both delight and agony, we are lovers indeed.

Similarly, the claim that "God is love" makes more sense when we understand love as the ability to embrace the other even when they disappoint us and cause pain. The Hebrew prophets, particularly Hosea, portray God as not able to walk away from the beloved who damages the relationship. St. Paul reminded early Christians that "while we were yet sinners, God loved us." God's love embraces us totally, not conditionally, and it is a life-long task to internalize that truth.

Another thought is even more challenging. From our point of view, God sometimes disappoints us, and that has to be acknowledged. Life is often very, very difficult, even tragic. Here Jewish spirituality has something to teach Christians: part of the journey of faith includes putting up with a deity who does not seem to play by the rules he is said to have laid down. Still loving a God who sometimes seems to us an underachiever is not a small thing.

At the same time, those who love God know what Job means when he says, "Even if he slay me, yet will I love him." Those whose spirituality has been touched by even the briefest taste of ecstasy stay in the relationship despite the fact that God, like any beloved other, is finally unknowable, uncontrollable.

Whether with the prophets we see God's own suffering in relationship with Israel, or with the apostles see on the Cross God's suffering in relation to the entire human race, something about a holiday marked by images of hearts shot through with arrows touches us deeply. Beyond the candy and the canoodling, our celebration of romantic love this month reminds us that mature spirituality and mature love are much alike, each embracing an Other who is a source of both pain and great joy.

## Lovers and Friends: The Ultimate Human Communion

June, the traditional month for brides, calls to mind the Bible's great love song, one of its least known books.

The Song of Songs, sometimes called the Song of Solomon, is unique among the sacred books of Judaism, Christianity, and Islam. It is the only book where a woman speaks in her own voice, rather than having her words reported by a narrator. It is the only book to report anything of the inner life of a woman in love.

In this book, a woman is the protagonist; she is her beloved's equal; she even shares her remarkable dream life with us. How tradition came to speak of the Song of Songs as written by Solomon is a mystery.

The book does not mount a sustained argument. It depicts confusion at times—it's a picture of passion. The lovers revel in nature; they have a sense of play; they tease and they delight in waiting.

I would not hide this book from teenagers. Its main tension comes from longing: waiting for the right person, time, and place. Books and movies in our day deal with passion by having folks go to bed (if a bed is even used) at the earliest possible moment. Here there is none of that, nothing casual, but elaborate courting, giving the erotic all the attention it is due.

The main reason I would have young people and everyone contemplating marriage read this book is that neither the man nor the woman is the dominant party in the relationship: they do not control, dominate, or subjugate each other. They meet as equals as they court, tease, and entice each other.

No one person has to do all the work in making the love happen. No one person has to make all the effort to make the relationship playful. They delight in each other without seeking to control.

The modern reader will never relax with the ancient compliments about a lover who is likened to a goat, or remarkable for having all her teeth!

The modern reader is, however, helpfully struck that, amid all the passionate talk, the description the male lover most often uses for the woman is "my friend." And certainly the playful talk of climbing the palm tree will make us giggle as surely as it did the unknown woman of the ancient Middle East.

Love poetry is powerful—we are aware of rabbis who were upset about the popularity of the book and Christian monks who spiritualized its content away. Jews and Christians have been nervous about this book—no other Hebrew book has had more books written about it.

The celebration of the physical has been hard for some people to take—but think back to Genesis and the "very, very good" God stamps on the world, especially the animate world. The Song of Songs repeatedly and deliberately takes the reader back to the original garden.

We have friends and we have lovers. The ideal expression of love is with someone who is both. The Song of Songs celebrates the ultimate human communion for careful and patient lovers.

Many have guessed about why and how this book got into anyone's Bible. It is a book to be cherished by religious people as the owner's manual for the human body and its emotional component.

How to be a lover without being oppressor or victim, how to take the risks, and how to play remain questions that go to the heart of our existence. The Song of Songs reminds us of the glorious possibilities.

# CHAPTER FOUR
## Public Issues

### America's Other Moral Crisis

Those of us who celebrate Christmas do well to remember that Jesus of Nazareth was not an educated liberal who happened to "identify with" the poor. Jesus *was* poor. In fact, the rural peasant trade he practiced generated less income than it took to support an urban slave in those days. Jesus is portrayed in the gospels as commenting on money more than any other social issue. He came by this issue honestly, and occasionally felt it important to point out to people that in a culture where participation in "the Land" is everything, he had no place to call his own.

We have missed something of the edge that was deliberately put into the story of Jesus' birth. As it has become familiar, it has lost its shock value. "There was no room for them" in the inn meant for Mary and Joseph, as it does now, that their kind was not welcome in decent hotels. Stables were and are squalid and unsanitary places to have a baby. Feed boxes do not make soft cradles.

In case we miss the point, the familiar story has Jesus' birth announced not to the elite but to shepherds working the night shift. Minimum wage workers whose occupation left them unclean for most purposes in their culture, they were on the very edges of society. To them the news of great joy is announced.

We should not be surprised at this turn of events. Mary, when told she would bear the Messiah, sang: "He has put down the mighty from their seats and the rich he has sent empty away." There is no reason to doubt that she meant it. There is no escaping it. If you simply take the stories of what Jesus says and does, and add them up, he thought the compelling moral issue of his time was how those who had wealth and power treated those who did not. Jesus was on the side of the outsider.

In my lifetime no religious group has more clearly expressed the consequences of these simple and obvious facts than the U.S. Conference of Catholic Bishops. In 1986 they laid out a few fundamental conclusions that could have been written yesterday—and could well have been repeated in the months leading to the recent elections.

Among the principles they laid down were: "Every economic decision and institution must be judged in light of whether it protects or undermines the dignity of human persons. . . . All members of society have a special obligation to the poor and vulnerable. . . . Human rights are the minimum for life in community. . . . Society as a whole, acting through public and private institutions, has the moral responsibility to enhance human dignity and protect human rights."

How petty seem the allegedly moral concerns trumpeted in the last months by Protestants and Catholics alike when compared with those magnificent values. We live in a country where we believe we can have wars without raising taxes, where deficits are climbing, where the "privatizing" of social programs will put our children and their children under tremendous burdens. Nonetheless, like those rearranging deck chairs on the *Titanic*, we have filled our discussions in the last months with questions having to do with private rather than public life.

There certainly is a moral crisis in America: it is that we don't recognize the real moral crisis in America. Perhaps remembering the realities of Jesus' birth and life will correct our shortsightedness.

## Scoundrels Hijack Our Values

When Samuel Johnson observed in 1775 that "patriotism is the last refuge of the scoundrel," he was disapproving of scoundrels, not patriotism. What scoundrels did, and do, is hijack people's values in order to amass power and wealth for themselves. It is not just patriotism that is used this way, but anything that evokes people's fear of losing what is sacred to them. Family and moral values are recent examples of values being hijacked for ignoble purposes.

When the two can't be told apart, religion is as bad as politics. No religion on earth fails to have blood on its hands—the arguments tend to boil down to whose religion has more. No fictional example of the moral profiteer is more memorable than Professor Harold Hill of *The Music Man*, who sells musical instruments and band uniforms by harnessing people's fear that their youth may be corrupted by the presence of a pool table. No real-life example is more horrific than what happened in Europe when an evil man convinced Germans that they were victims of a conspiracy in the 1930s.

What will history say of our own time?

Eric Fromm, who gave much of his career to helping people live and love authentically, observed: "There is perhaps no phenomenon which contains so much destructive feeling as moral indignation, which permits envy or hate to be acted out under the guise of virtue."

History provides an example. The Crusades, no matter what the motivation of their initiators, became the opportunity for breathtaking pillage and murder. Can anyone say that the love of God motivated those crimes? Of course not, but those who perpetrated them said so. Some of them apparently believed it.

Fromm and Johnson suggest a test for weighing our responses to what we see and hear. If someone consistently raises our fears and repeatedly harks on what is wrong in an effort to get our votes or our money, we may be in the presence of a scoundrel.

If someone reduces patriotism or morality to one issue or a very small cluster of issues, a scoundrel may be at work. If we notice that our outrage can be linked to our own sense of personal security or to our pocketbooks, we may be listening to a scoundrel.

That's the easy part—if the alarms just described go off, don't vote for the scoundrels and don't give them money. The more challenging part is regulation of whatever, inside our own souls, makes us vulnerable to the scoundrel's pitch. Fromm says that the envy and hate on which the scoundrel relies are already there. The scoundrel merely provides the channel through which they can flow.

It is worth asking ourselves, when we hear a stirring denunciation of someone else, what in us makes us interested in hearing such things? An answer comes in part from the fact that we tend to blame in others what we fear in ourselves. This may explain why so many high-profile crusaders turn out to have secretly sordid lives. Those who are willing to look into the chaos of their own souls tend to give others a break. People who know their lives to be in order are seldom obsessed with apparent disorder in the lives of others.

The highest use of religion is not to create the illusion of order and a place from which to obsess about the failings of those around us. The highest use of religion is to make us enough at peace with our own dark places that there is no joy in degrading others. Such a state of things would put a lot of scoundrels out of work, but it would be pleasant.

---

## Littleton: A Time for Examination

I started my professional life as a high school teacher. Anyone who has spent time with young people in what are for most of us the most difficult years cannot but agonize at the thought of those young bodies lying limp on the library floor in Littleton, Colorado.

### Examine the Culture

What has caused additional agony is the flood of agenda running that has followed this tragedy. It seems that each writer knows that if only his or her theory had been followed, this tragedy could have been prevented. Religious people have not been absent among those with easy answers.

The more we learn about the violence in Littleton, however, the more complex the problem appears, and it seems that we will have to take a fearless and thorough look at our entire culture. What stands in the way of looking at how the totality of our culture shaped these horrible events seems to be our American addiction to blame, denial, and displacement.

### Blame

There is something comforting about knowing whom to blame. It's almost magical: anxiety disappears when we know whose fault something is. Knowing whom to blame provides a sense of closure, and, more important, makes it clear that somebody other than ourselves is responsible for what has gone wrong.

As I surf the Net, I see working mothers, the NRA, permissive school officials, the entertainment industry, and even the gay community blamed for Littleton. In each case the impression is left that one particular group is responsible for what occurred.

The times call for us to suspend blaming (and the relief it brings), and take inventory of the factors in our nation's life that produce violence such as daily road rage and the extraordinary horror we still grieve over in Colorado.

### Denial

Denial has been popping up every day since the first reports from Columbine School.

Some people seem to dismiss everything from the St. Valentine's Day Massacre to My Lai as an aberration, and urge us to think about all the good people. Gun fanciers have been quick to point out that only two-tenths of one percent of all guns in the country are used in committing crime, as if that settled the gun question.

Usually very wise representatives of the women's movement seem unable to concede the possibility that the progress and justice women have achieved in recent years may have had some fallout on the way children develop. Fathers and mothers need to examine their parenting.

No one is willing to admit that their cause—or their usual way of doing things—might have some tiny downside. And so we have a kind of impasse, with progress prevented because of our difficulty in seeing the gray in most situations and then working together to correct it.

*Displacement*

Our national tendency toward displacement is equally insidious. We know people who think they can save their marriage by having a child rather than by working on their relationship—and we pity such a child. If we let Littleton be about guns or parenting or school security alone, we lose the opportunity to identify and work on the complex of issues that erode our national life. A sneaky form of displacement is the Rodney King syndrome, the mistaken belief that all that is required is for each person to try to be a little nicer to everyone, with no requirement to examine and overhaul values.

*A Watershed*

While there is no way to find a silver lining in the tragedy of Littleton, and certainly no way to kid ourselves with rosy talk about people not "dying in vain," whatever that means, we have once again as a nation received a wake-up call. If ever there was a time for a careful examination of how young people's personalities are formed in our communities and schools, this is it.

The question before us is whether we will tether our sacred cows and set aside our financial and personal priorities long enough to look at the factors that threaten to destroy us as a people. At no time since the Civil War have we stood at such a watershed.

## Cloning: Can We Think Together?

Who owns clones? Will cloned human beings possess civil rights? May we create deformed clones for scientific study, and kill clones whose scientific usefulness has ceased? What about other species? Should scientific protocols regarding the treatment of research animals have the force of law? Researchers recently cloned some fifty mice. Because they have said the cloning of humans is imminent, I want to offer a few thoughts and questions.

This is not forbidden territory. Some religious people in the public and private sectors have somewhat hysterically opposed certain kinds of inquiry and technological application, anything that appears to trespass on God's turf. Reading the Bible in its total context, I do not understand such a position, though I do understand that the cruelest forms of racism and other oppression have been excused by citing particular Scriptures without context.

When kindly Augustinian monk Gregor Mendel invented and named genetics through his manipulation of plant reproduction, he had no sense of himself interfering in God's business. The practical implications of applied genetic research are in fact very exciting.

The thought of eliminating unfortunate or lethal aspects of one's makeup by the addition of a carefully aimed "virus" that will minutely alter genetic structure is now thinkable. Beyond that, in the realm of the brain as much as other organs or systems, finding ways to develop what humans can fully become, individually and as a group, is about as exciting a concept as one can imagine. We must admit that to reach a stage in evolution where a species can consciously participate in its development is to come to a moment that can be one of awe, possibility, or horror. The dream of philosophers and theologians, ancient and modern, is also the nightmare of Hitler's "master race" and the racist eugenics of Margaret Sanger.

A few years ago great objection was raised to the use by contemporary science of data collected in the Nazi concentration camps. The objection, besides all revulsion that the word "Nazi" rightly evokes, was that human subjects were subjected to experiments against their will. We have come slowly and painfully to agreement that each human being possesses rights, including the right not to be seized and subjected to experiments.

Principles about free and informed consent to human experimentation protect people who already exist. What principles protect people we might create? No one supposes that the first human clone will be patted on the head, given to an Iowa couple to raise in privacy, sent out to play, to school, and off to whatever life it chooses. One imagines instead that it would be closely monitored from conception to autopsy. It is hard to imagine it making choices at all, though choice making is what freedom boils down to.

Before any clones are brought to birth, one imagines many thousands of clone embryos studied and disposed of. When there is no mother's privacy to protect, what are the issues about use and disposal of a human embryo? The careful and resolute agnosticism of *Roe v. Wade* about the nature of the earliest stages of human development was meant to leave the moral question to individuals and their physicians, but it has instead ironically encouraged in the popular mind the notion that there is nothing to ask. Cloning will ask it again in less complicated ways.

The urge to know is powerful: in practice human cloning cannot be prevented. On the road to perfecting ourselves through the data that human cloning will bring, human life may be brought into existence for scientific servitude. I am concerned about that.

As a society we are far from able to legislate wisely regarding genetic work; before legislation, we need conversation. The conversation that should occur in the culture needs to involve those who lead the way in research and those who are specially trained to work with moral and ethical issues. There are think tanks and institutes where this conversation goes on among experts. The claim that human cloning is imminent requires that we all become interested in the conversation if our leaders are to make choices based on public thinking rather than public outcry.

## The Last of the Good Negroes

As a child in the 1950s, I was regularly assured by my pastor and school teachers not to be too worried about the civil rights movement: "Remember, there are still a lot of good Negroes." In the all-white Smoketown Elementary School outside of Lancaster, this theme was repeated often enough that, as an adult, I recognize that we kids were not the ones the teacher was trying to reassure.

"Good Negroes," of course, meant African Americans who did not demand equal justice and who acted, sounded, and looked like their cultural values were those of the European American majority. They were "Good Negroes" if they did not want to be people in their own right, if they did not threaten the notion that white is best. They were good because they stayed in the invisible place the majority, northern as well as southern, assigned them.

In February, when America tries to strengthen its memory of the strength, struggles, and contributions of those of African descent, I am thankful that there were in the long run so few of the "Good Negroes" my pastor and teachers hoped for.

All Americans are richer because resistance to oppression continued and grew. All Americans are richer because we are aware of the contributions of African Americans to our culture. All Americans are richer because the entire society receives the gifts of men and women who became able to contribute their gifts and talents to our workforce and national life.

Someday, perhaps, Americans will see fulfilled what the civil rights movement began. It is not clear to me that the struggle against racism gets the attention in media, the work-place, and religious institutions that it once did. I find that when I mention it in sermons there is barely a look of recognition on most faces—as though, yes, they heard about that once.

My concern this February is the ghost of the "Good Negro." It was never put to rest. It rose again when the women's movement began to touch the churches. Some people, who were prepared to put up with women clergy if they had to, drew the line at hearing the particular insights of women presented as if they had something unique to contribute to religious understanding. (They did have, of course.) People found themselves saying what Henry Higgins said in *My Fair Lady*: "Why can't a woman be more like a man?" A "good" woman priest was to act like a man, preach like a man, and certainly not pretend that she brought anything new to our common experience. It was all chillingly familiar.

This short column cannot explore all of the issues that arise in religious groups over questions about gays and lesbians. As I participate in discussions of the issues, I hear one thing that takes me back to 1956 in Smoketown.

People will actually say they "don't mind" if gays and lesbians come to church and sit in the pews, but they are offended that they would "rub our faces in it."

When I ask what that means, what comes is that it is offensive when "they" want their identity, values, and relationship recognized like anyone else's. Even more troubling for some people is the idea that gays or lesbians might have gained from their experience of God religious insights to share with the majority of those in the pews.

There is little these thoughts have to say to those who do not recognize members of other races, members of the opposite sex, or gays and lesbians as people of worth. For the rest of us, however, Black History Month is a good time to ask if we really believe that God's Spirit fills the whole world, and if those whose experience is very different from ours do not really have a great deal to give us—once they stop being "good"?

## Elected Officials Need Vision

Because my diocese covers fourteen counties, our parishioners interact with many state legislators and senators when the situation calls for it. Not long ago I joined 130 parishioners in Harrisburg to visit lawmakers from our eastern and northeastern Pennsylvania counties on a matter with a high moral impact. We were received well and listened to by some highly motivated women and men—with one appalling exception.

A state senator, who couldn't be bothered to put his jacket on to receive his constituents, listened with too-obvious impatience as we made our case and urged him to do what was best for the entire commonwealth and its future.

"Yes, yes," he then said, "but if this doesn't bring money to X County, I'm not interested."

Hearts do sink into the pits of stomachs, and mine did. This man is fairly young, apparently full of ambition, and yet totally clueless about his job. He was not elected to be nothing more than a pork butcher for his county. He was elected to help rule one of the few states in the country that calls itself a commonwealth, an entity organized for the common good.

We elect people to represent our local interests in part, of course, but the welfare of the entire commonwealth is a matter of local interest. We elect people to have a share in the governance of the whole state. This man could not see beyond his nose. Nothing we said could make a dent in his patronizing attitude.

There are people who do not recognize the difference between political questions and moral issues. It is a moral issue when a lawmaker has no vision beyond the amount of cash a decision will deliver to his constituents in the short term and no reluctance about saying that to concerned constituents. It is a moral outrage that he is so crassly focused on pork instead of the common good. It is stunningly unstatesman-like behavior.

He was a startling contrast to senators and representatives I met in Washington on a trip seeking aid for the Christian victims of genocide in Sudan. I encountered one midwestern senator who was not only willing to put his career on the line for powerless people, but was doing so cheerfully. He was a person whose vision extended far beyond questions of pork.

"Where there is no vision, the people perish," says a familiar passage in the Hebrew Scriptures. It is a step from the original context, focused on vision from God, to the question of national or state vision—but not a big step. Where elected officials do not have their minds on something greater than themselves, something more than the (necessary) acquisition and maintenance of political power, nothing much happens, and people suffer.

If we consider a great Democrat, Franklin Delano Roosevelt, and a great Republican, Abraham Lincoln, we see people who knew how to get into office and how to stay there. But we see something else, a concern that transcended self-interest, a search for a greater good, an inkling of such good that the prophet called it vision.

In our society we cannot expect that persons who ask for our vote should share our creed. What people of good will have every right to demand of those who seek the power and privileges that elected office brings, however, is that they have some vision beyond the grotesquely crass—some striving for long-term good for the whole people.

The biblical idea that where there is a lack of vision the people die is far too serious an observation about human events for us, who believe, to let any public servant forget it.

## Strong Religious Belief: Sick or Healthy

The psychological world once listed "strong religious belief" in its official diagnostic manual. It was removed from the list of diseases in the early 1990s. With contemporary neurological researchers and St. Paul, I wonder about that decision. Some religious attitudes and beliefs may have little to do with health.

Andrew Newberg and Eugene d'Aquili, medical researchers, have done neurological research into spiritual experience and brain functioning. They reported their findings in *Why God Won't Go Away* (Ballantine Books, 2002). Not themselves religious people, they were surprised to discover physical evidence that our brains work differently, in some senses better, when we engage in spiritual activity. They ask the question science itself cannot answer, whether we are in some sense made for communion with the divine. Along the way, the authors review the physical health benefits of spiritual practice. They are not shy about the differences, overall, in everything from marital happiness to longevity in those who walk the road less traveled.

So far, so good. As a professional in the religious world, I find it reassuring to know that there is evidence that what I try to help people find is in every sense good for them. I have nonetheless always been troubled by extremists, people whose "strong religious belief" puts chips on their shoulders that can make them, sadly, everything from pests to terrorists. It is not easily forgotten that the perpetrators of 9/11 died with religious language on their lips.

Newberg and d'Aquili take up this question in trying to separate genuinely mystical from delusional experience. They provide an interesting secular test to distinguish between healthy spiritual experience and something unhealthy, even psychotic. They find people whose religious experience is healthy to be characterized by joy, serenity, and wholeness, by "loss of pride and ego, a quieting of the mind, and an emptying of the self." Those whose religion tends toward the delusional, however, are marked by fearfulness, isolation from others, "grandiosity and egotistical importance."

The authors were looking for psychological, not theological, criteria, but there was for me an overwhelming shock of recognition when I read their words. When St. Paul wrote to the embattled community of believers in Galatia two millennia ago he made a similar point.

Paul's contrast was "flesh," the baseness that leads to chaos and destruction, versus "spirit," life in communion with God the redeemer. After observing that morality is summed up in "you shall love your neighbor as yourself," Paul came up with a test to let people know which force was governing their lives. His test was practical, not doctrinal. He lists fifteen symptoms of unspiritual living, and includes our doctors' list as he mentions "enmities, strife, jealousy, anger, quarrels, dissentions, factions." Among his list of indicators of spiritual living: "joy, peace, patience, kindness . . . gentleness, and self-control." The choice to live the spiritual life, Paul concludes, is a daily battle and choice to put to death the base urges.

If one's religion tends to lead to or reinforce one's feelings of superiority, arrogance, hostility, fighting, and so on, both the apostle and the psychologist (for perhaps different reasons) think something is wrong. All religions I know about have divisions and disagreements, just as points of view differ in science, law, and in every walk of life. Religious people are caught in a double bind, however: disagreements that include swaggering, demonizing of others, and an inner state of turmoil just are not spiritual, and, if the doctors are right, could indicate something much worse.

St. Paul or modern researchers: people of faith have concrete ways both to measure how their faith is working for them and to move toward wholeness.

## Getting over the Pursuit of Happiness

A couple of years ago I lost the core of what had been my happiness, and it is not coming back in any future I can see. On a daily basis I was experiencing that loss as a hole in my interior, a persistent aching lack. For the first time in my life I felt utterly bereft.

In struggling to get that happiness back I resorted to every avenue you would expect in pursuing it: prayer, counseling, new activities, novel strategies, etc. Nada. Then, when a student in my class at Muhlenberg College asked a question about "the meaning of life," I remembered what I once used to know. The pursuit of happiness is in itself always a mistake. When happiness is pursued, like a dog or a small child, it runs away.

The student's question reminded me of the book that was very popular when I was a student, Viktor Frankl's *Man's Search for Meaning*. There Frankl reflected on his concentration camp years and discovered something about those prisoners who did not just sicken and die as many did: they retained meaning in their lives.

How could those who were stripped of everything and brutalized on a daily basis ever claim that their lives retained meaning? Frankl insisted that it is each person's vocation to assign meaning to his or her life, whatever its circumstances. From my point of view, how one assigns meaning to one's life is one's essential spirituality.

Death camp inmates, Frankl found, survived when they assigned meaning to their lives by remaining compassionate, helpful, and caring in an environment that extinguished those qualities in most people. Even when the moment came that others took away one's life, he says, one could still choose to reflect human dignity.

Remembering Frankl enabled me once again to throw off the chief delusion of my generation, that happiness is the goal of living. In refocusing my mental energy on the meaning and purpose I assign to my life, there came a new sense of centeredness and calm. Having a focus on purpose has enabled me to speak somewhat boldly about things that could be costly in the long the run: what matters is the mission.

A kind of haze is lifting as I consider this chain of events. Somewhere in the last twenty years my idealism was supplanted in my deepest self by the yuppie illusion that happiness can be pursued, captured, held on to—and even measured. When it departed, I encountered what I thought was emotional poverty.

This surprises me. As a believer and a member of the clergy, I have said the right words and, in fact, believed them, about the purpose of existence. I certainly have pursued important goals, but never had to do that without the training wheels provided by the measure of happiness I've recently lost. I have, in fact, been getting along with both meaning and happiness all these years.

The training wheels are gone now and to my surprise I find I can ride: without a ghost of a chance of controlling happiness, I know the importance of meaning, and it is more than enough. It makes one in some sense fearless.

I can never claim to have had a death camp experience: that would debase the memory of the millions who died around young Viktor Frankl. I have, very late in life, had an experience of deprivation sufficient to drive me to find where my heart really lies. I am driven to admit that I wish I had suffered more, and sooner, but with St. Paul I suspect that we are not given more than we can handle.

## Unsung Heroes All around Us

It was billed as a hip-hop Mass: rap, dork dancing, busy lighting, and unimaginably loud music. Contrary to the expectations of some of my fellow geezers, it was also thoroughly orthodox in religious content.

It was refreshing and hopeful to encounter thirteen hundred young people putting so much energy into expressing their faith in the sounds and sights of their generation. We had *Jesus Christ Superstar*, they have rap. Many young people there had a kind of Pentecost experience, hearing the good news in their own language for the first time.

Something else impressed me. For the young people gathered at the Episcopal Youth Event in Berea, Kentucky, the awesome moment was possible in part because over a hundred adult volunteers were putting in eight consecutive sixteen-hour days. Most gave up vacations and paid their own expenses. Beyond that gathering, throughout the summer, other young people have also been having life-changing experiences because volunteers are invested in the future of our youth.

Despite our reputation for living in selfish times, IndependentSector.org, tells us that 109 million American adults volunteer 19.9 billion hours a year without compensation. The Web site estimates the dollar value at $225.9 billion.

Much of the quality of American life depends on people who volunteer. Cultural, charitable, and religious institutions rely heavily on individuals who extend themselves for others. Think of the people in your block and the activities and causes to which they give themselves. It's a good corrective for cynicism.

Part of the irreducible minimum of healthy spirituality is connectedness with the world and commitment to its wellness. For those who think in other terms, natural selection seems to favor such a sense of connectedness and altruism because it helps insure the survival and progress of our species. Both points of view seem correct. Either way, however, the results are good for the individual and the community.

Quietly knitting for the indigent, putting together a flyer for Scouts, working in volunteer construction crews are activities that vary in noise and camaraderie, but they share a commitment to our common life, expressing human solidarity on the most basic level. It suggests the "muscle memory" athletes and musicians depend upon: what you do becomes part of you.

It may be interesting to speculate on what spiritual wounds would keep a person from investing energy in others. The cure, however, may be of more interest than the diagnosis. Web surfing reveals studies that highlight the mental and physical benefits of giving time and self for others.

There may also be something redemptive in taking time and giving it away, a kind of a defiant thrust against a culture of endless busyness. It saves money, too: those who shop out of boredom or addiction discover that you can't shop and deliver meals at the same time.

Readers of this column know that one of my concerns is reaching for the highest rather than the lowest common denominator among the spiritualities present in our community. Low-key summer reflection on the phenomenon of the volunteer allows us to affirm together how working for the good of others reflects a sense of life's basic characteristic as a gift.

It is a gift with challenges. In helping each other meet them we discover ourselves. In responding to each other by expending time and energy, by showing up for each other, we offer something back to the source of our life and we are enriched.

When the ancient writer James told his readers that "true religion" meant visiting the sick and caring for the widow and orphan, he was telling us that the core of all faith is connectedness with others, a connectedness learned by doing and only feebly celebrated in words such as these.

# Let's Have More Adult Content

When a cable-TV movie begins with a notice about "adult situations" or "adult language," we know we will see depictions of sex that appeal to adolescents unaware of the importance of relationship—or at least fore-play!—in sexual intimacy. We know also that, rather than the words of adults who love and use language creatively, we will hear a limited list of mindless adjectives and verbs.

On the simplest level, we learn to decode "adult language" and "adult content" as meaning "Beavis and Butt-head will think this is neat," and we take it in stride. But on another level there is an absence of adult content in American film that is not so easily overlooked, and that is the substitution of feeling tone for ideas as a shortcut to the resolution of problems.

Films that resolve historical or moral issues by manipulating the emotions of the audience are unsatisfying in that we are not asked to *think* about the motives and ideas of characters. Motives and ideas lie largely undisclosed in American film. Religious principle, particularly Christian religious principle, is unexplored, if mentioned at all.

Regrettably, Steven Spielberg's *Amistad* provides an example, as do his previous *Schindler's List* and *The Color Purple*. Spielberg could move from being an enormously successful filmmaker, without leaving the entertainment business, and become a great one as well, if his characters could invite us into their thoughts and motives.

I write this piece in New Haven, Connecticut, where the *Amistad* story is an important piece of local history, and has been for decades. Here people experience a kind of surprised numbness about the filmed account.

Among the surprises is the reaction of Congregationalists. They are concerned that their religious tradition is reduced to a sentimental joke at one point in the movie. They are much more distressed that the religious principles that guided American and English abolitionists are not disclosed, let alone explored. Once again we see people acting from deep personal convictions, but are not told what those convictions are. Christianity is distilled down to feelings of generalized compassion, hardly the only arrow in the abolitionist quiver.

Abolitionists took seriously a *theological claim* of the kind the Declaration of Independence makes, that God creates everyone with equal dignity and worth, and that God gives each person rights that no lesser judge dare abridge. That the author of those words, Mr. Jefferson, did not free his own slaves until his death illustrates the complexity of human resolve, and our slowness to realize the implications of our deepest insights (ask the suffragists).

Not giving real attention to the underlying principles of the New England abolitionists streamlines Spielberg's film. It also feeds our national amnesia about the role of religion in public life. Every January we hear of Dr. Martin Luther King Jr., stripped of "the Reverend" and presented without attention paid to his own motives and rhetoric as they were shaped by Christianity. Worse, we are asked to ignore the power of the black church, often the sole unifying and empowering institution in a world hostile to African Americans.

If you do not believe that the story of our national origins has been detheologized by the revisionist historians of the last two generations, try to guess the author and occasion of the following words. "Let us with caution indulge the supposition that morality can be maintained without religion. Whatever may be conceded to the influence of refined education on minds of peculiar structure, reason and experience both forbid us to expect that national morality can prevail in exclusion of religious principle."

The words are of those of George Washington, at his Farewell Address upon leaving the presidency, with nothing to gain from saying them. I commend them to serious filmmakers, at least for discussion.

## Our Duty to Oppose War in Iraq

When you read this, we may already be at war. As I write from the late-winter meeting of the bishops of the Episcopal Church, Congress is about to begin debate on preemptive measures against Iraq. Our discussion has been intense, and we recognize that our first duty is to call people to prayer for our country and the world. Prayer, however, leads us to witness to our moral commitments.

With the leaders of the Evangelical Lutheran Church in America, the Presbyterian Church of the USA, the Orthodox Church in America, and the U. S. Conference of Catholic Bishops—among others—we find that we have a duty to oppose a war.

Since September 11, 2001, the United States, together with other nations, has attempted to heighten world security through focused activity against Al-Qaeda and other terrorist organizations. We support these efforts for the sake of the human family. We are not soft on Iraq. The brutality and overall evil of the Saddam Hussein regime stand condemned before the world. So, why do we hesitate?

Like many people of good will, we consider war a last resort. In fact, all Episcopalians formally and regularly commit themselves "to strive for justice and peace among all people." We believe that restraint and continued commitment to international cooperation provide the path to lasting peace. Our concern is not just for the elimination of terrorism, but the elimination of the conditions that produce it.

Martin Luther King once observed that "violence is the cry of the unheard." We must never condone terrorism, but we are fools if we do not seek to understand its causes.

War is sometimes unavoidable, but at this point it is hard to see how a war with Iraq can be justified. Nobody claims that we have thoroughly pursued multilateral resolution of the matter. We have not even engaged in serious discussion of the possibility of economic sanctions to pressure Iraq to disarm. Worse still, a preemptive strike against Iraq and the degree of destruction necessary for clear and quick victory guarantee increased civilian casualties.

Without sufficient evidence of the need for us to defend ourselves, it is impossible to support the administration's moral choice to go to war, and a moral choice it is. The wiser moments of Christian and other spiritual traditions teach us to use the greatest prudence and caution when contemplating the use of lethal force.

We must accept the fact that the consequences of war with Iraq will not be contained within the borders of that country. Escalating the level of violence in the world virtually guarantees that the cycle of violence such as we have seen in Northern Ireland and Palestine will continue. Not all leaders have the maturity to accept this fact.

There are those in America who fight to keep "under God" in our pledge and "in God we trust" on the money. The country is festooned with "God Bless America" flags, bumper stickers, and baseball caps.

Issues of church and state aside, we must ask ourselves if we are prepared to take the hard look—at our nation, its economy, and its role in the world —that invoking God's name always demands. Those of us who grew up hearing "kill a Commie for Christ" brace ourselves for the hijacking of religious rhetoric in the next war.

As we continue to search for the perpetrators of the obscenity on September 11, 2001, we must maintain the perspective and discernment that keeps the United States free—and civilized.

## Women's Bodies: Exporting Cultural Homicide

It is difficult to think of one's own culture as harmful, but at times it is hard to evade such thoughts. My first clue that there might be a problem was reading in a report about an investigation into the immune system in the 1980s that many food allergies are almost totally unknown in poor or famine-stricken countries. They can't afford them.

I recently heard a physician reviewing the evidence that anorexia and other eating disorders were almost unknown in non-Western cultures. As those cultures have achieved economic success and Western advertising has entered their lives, women have begun to hate their bodies and begun to starve themselves. The effect our culture is having on other cultures today makes our previous gift of smallpox-infested blankets to Native Americans appear relatively benign.

To check myself out, I hauled my undergraduate art history text (Janson) off a shelf in the basement, and looked at the women of three millennia, clothed or not. Such a survey leads one to make a choice on how to understand the body. Either liposuction is the salvation of the world, or nature intends most women to be soft, fleshy, perhaps even zaftig.

For most of human history the female image was portrayed more or less realistically. Even the artificially flat-chested flappers of the 1920s sported thighs and calves that would be unfashionable today. Fashion is not the point, of course. Fatty tissue is related to healthy levels of estrogen, and it has been suggested by more than one health authority that women do well to carry a little weight after menopause, for the sake of the hormone balance necessary for good physical and mental health. Starving oneself and ingesting artificially produced hormones is only a weak second choice to letting the body function normally.

The situation can be even worse for younger women: most Americans can remember the tragic end of singer Karen Carpenter, whose obsession with not eating caused the fatal deterioration of her heart.

It may be worth investigating how our culture reinforces the image of the emaciated female. To what extent must modern men consider their complicity in images that diminish the life experience of women? Perhaps fashion advertising needs to be regulated in the same way tobacco ads are controlled: "The Surgeon General has determined that undernourishing the human body can lead to organ damage or death."

None of this is a justification for obesity, but a call for reason about the normal proportions, and the normal variety of the human shape.

The reader may wonder what any of this has to do with religion. In the first place, of course, is the moral objection to cultural norms that cause women to hate themselves or even die. That is a kind of cultural homicide; at the very least, it is what a writer of my youth called "soul murder."

The positive "not for women only" point is even more important. In the Hebrew Scriptures, revered by Jews, Christians, and Muslims, God's creation of the human body with all its variety of form is called "good." People who can feel positively about their physical selves, who can be grateful for the gift of the bodies they actually have, can enjoy their physicality, their lives. Those attitudes of gratitude and joy would be cultural values well worth exporting.

## A Positive Tax Revolt

Home Depot and Sam's Club are doing it. Many other retailers may be doing it. Customers can spend their three-hundred-dollar tax rebate checks without ever depositing or cashing them. Just sign them over.

At the Episcopal diocese of Bethlehem, we are offering a similar service. You may want to consider offering the service at your church, synagogue, temple, or mosque as well.

The tax rebates are giving back revenues that could have funded children's programs or health-care initiatives. The rebates and the recent reforms in the tax and estate tax laws may push us further toward a two-class society. That is a trend about which opinions vary. Some think the rebate program is a good thing; others do not.

My sense of what is "enough" and what constitutes "wealth" has been permanently altered by a visit to Swaziland where I experienced Third World poverty and illness. Seeing people living in shelters scraped out of the dirt—to discover later that they were school teachers—increased my profound gratitude to be an American.

It also heightened my sense of my Christian responsibility to share. Knowing also that adults and children in our partner diocese of Kajo-Keji in southern Sudan are dying of starvation elicits my compassion—and my anger: since the beginning of the last century, famine is almost always the result of political decisions that can only be described as evil.

I do not know what others are doing with their rebate checks, but Diana and I are dividing ours between New Bethany Ministries in Bethlehem and famine relief for Kajo-Keji. I invite you to share your windfall in a ministry of compassion. What an interesting dinner-time conversation with the family, deciding whom to help.

Deciding not to have things so that others can eat is an ancient religious discipline. Christianity's early development as an urban religion included a feeding program for the poor as an essential part of its program.

We read in our Scriptures that the institution of deacons arose out of the Church in Jerusalem's intent to make sure that the ministry to the poor was carried out fairly. Part of the deacon's job is to remind us that it is a fundamental part of Christian discipleship to deny ourselves so that others may merely survive.

I have indicated to our parishioners that they can simply endorse their checks to Diocese of Bethlehem with a word or line indicating what cause they want to support. We will forward money for foreign relief through Episcopal Relief and Development and cut checks for total amounts for ministries to the poor and marginalized in various parts of our fourteen counties.

Those who have already deposited their checks may, of course, send similar amounts or a tithe in the same way. Three hundred dollars is not a fortune. Multiplied by the taxpayers who read this, however, many millions of dollars can help people whose need we can barely imagine.

As I write, "tax revolt" comes to mind. That has to do, though, with people taking action to lower their taxes. The suggestion here is that we take action to counter the culture of "having" with a witness for "sharing."

For those of us with empty nests, it is easier to just do without the checks entirely. For others a tithe may be what is practical. But let's all do something with this unbudgeted income to care for others and to give a silent witness to the people in government and the news media who are watching where that money is spent.

## The Shepard Murder: Words Are a Lens

Like most semipublic figures, I get an occasional piece of hate mail. It comes with the territory, and one lives with it with varying degrees of peace.

A letter I received after the brutal murder of Matthew Shepard troubled me deeply because of its stark reminder of the element of evil that can be present in the people identified as good in any society.

Matthew was a young and active Episcopalian. At least part of the motive for the crime was the fact that he was openly homosexual. My correspondent was outraged at the attention being paid to this hate crime, and went on to say that if someone is gay, he is taking the risk that things like this will happen.

Most arguments equating sexuality issues with civil rights and political issues are misleading, but there can be no doubt that here the shoe fits perfectly. That a person's ideas, color, sex, ethnicity, or sexuality should imply a heightened expectation of violent death or diminished protection of the law should be an abomination to anyone who subscribes to American political ideals, let alone a biblical notion of justice. History teaches otherwise, of course, but our problems are not just history.

As I travel around the fourteen counties of my diocese, eating in local restaurants and making purchases in local mini-marts, I routinely hear derogatory remarks made about Poles, Italians, and other ethnic groups. Language grows more intense however, when the group is made up of people whose behavior, even if private, is the subject of debate.

Our words create the lens through which people are seen. It is one thing to say that religious beliefs compel one to consider as sinful certain attitudes or behaviors. It is quite another to routinely speak of people in ways that label them as inferior human beings. Once a group has been classified as second-rate or worse, violence can and does follow.

Those of us who are somewhat conservative on moral questions need to be especially careful that our rhetoric does not become someone else's excuse for violence. Christians need to be even more careful about hauling out the platitude of "hate the sin but love the sinner." People who mouth those words often display very little love, especially when they utter them with a tone of superiority or with clenched jaws or fists.

There is another side to this concern for moderation in moral debate. Did you ever know anyone who was converted to your way of thinking because you insulted him? Perhaps you do, but I know no man or woman who ever experienced a change of mind or heart because someone belittled or expressed contempt for them or their way of thinking.

It is for practical as well as moral reasons that the New Testament urges us to be "speaking the truth in love." Insults do not convert anyone; usually they antagonize. Certainly people can be bullied or twisted with guilt to get them to change a policy or a behavior, but that change never lasts: that's why we have the word "backlash."

It seems that an important part of persuasion is drawing close to the person one wishes to persuade, finding as much common intellectual and personal ground as possible, and in that context introducing ideas or attitudes one wishes to advance. This method does not provide much ventilation for rage, of course, and being confronted with one's own anger may give one a powerful reality check—do I *really* love "the sinner"?

---

## Diversity Alone Kills: Patterns of Daily Action Make a People

We are becoming increasingly isolated from one another in America. The murder rate is up again. Racism is a worse problem than it was in 1970. More troubling still: neither observation is likely to get much of a response in casual conversation beyond shrugs of shoulders.

Despite what advocates of cultural diversity may say, diversity alone kills. Worldwide, the more homogeneous the population, the lower the crime rate. There have been years in the last decade when North Dakota had a murder rate of zero. It is also one of the least diverse states. The sad truth is that people tend to respect people they identify with. What makes systems of slavery and oppression work is the dehumanizing of those who are different. Diversity alone kills. What we need, of course, is diversity with respect, diversity with a sense of connection.

As we stand between Easter and Passover, whether we have deep religious convictions or none at all, there is something to be learned about people making. Passover and Easter have in common the recalling of saving events that each generation reclaims for itself as the center of its identity. This is done through ritual.

Ritual is the enacting of our deepest truths, at a level where mere words will not do the job. Telling a little child that you love him or her is one thing; a hug and a kiss are quite another. Doing all three together, combining words and actions, is the stuff of ritual. Jews tell the story as they praise God and share a symbolic meal. Christians do much the same. The combination of words and actions makes the people. Saying and doing symbolic things, treating one another as though we share values and history, makes a people of those who were no people.

I am not suggesting that all be forced to adopt one religious identity. I am arguing that if America is to profit from, rather than suffer because of its unavoidable diversity, we need rituals of commonality, interdependence, and respect. These need to be patterns of daily action that constantly reinforce the idea that we need and value one another.

Oddly enough, these rituals are at hand, although they have been largely discarded. "Good morning," and "How are you?" used to get in return, "Good morning," and "Fine, thanks. And you?" This was not an exchange of information; it was a ritual greeting, expressing concern for the other person's well-being. Only a recent immigrant would have thought it was a cue to talk about their lumbago. Try it today. All you get back is a clipped "I'm good," "I'm great," or something of the kind. There is no return greeting, and instead of the exchange of mutual regards, there is now a moment of fairly tedious self-assertion. Restoring the old pattern takes us out of ourselves, puts us into community with whoever greets us, whether they are of our race or ethnic background, or not. It is a ritual that gets at basics. Like all rituals, it accumulates value as it is repeated.

Equally basic is what an old commercial ritual did. You made your selection, took it to the cashier. The cashier rang it up, asked for "$9.50, please." You paid, and received your purchase with "Thank you," or even, "Thank you for shopping at Smith's." Now, if you are lucky, you get your purchase and "Have a nice day." Often you hear nothing at all, as if to thank you would demean the cashier.

Handing over a purchase with "Have a nice day" and "Thank you" are very different rituals. "Thank you" says that the seller needs the purchaser, of whatever background, and that we depend on one another for our common survival. It acknowledges that without buyers, cashiers and the firms who employ them do not eat. A mild affirmative from the buyer completed the ritual as an Amen completes a prayer.

This is not about etiquette. I am saying that if we force ourselves to enact simple values of respect and mutual dependence long enough and intensely enough, in what we do each day, respect for each other may well grow unconsciously and inevitably.

## Losing Innocence

The loss of innocence is a terrible moment in life, because the world changes permanently. My own story in this regard brings a twinge each October as preelection rhetoric invades every part of life.

It was a sweltering summer day in the East New York section of Brooklyn where I was working in a program for inner-city children—one of the few times in my life I did not mind the heat. President Johnson was about to sign the great Civil Rights Act.

The sense of joy and hope this piece of legislation evoked pushed the Vietnam War and many other concerns out of consciousness for a time. America was about to get a long-needed overhaul. It was a moment to believe in our leaders.

Then came shock, pain, and terrible confusion. Among the sections that would guarantee basic dignity and fair play to every American was the provision that came like a physical blow. The Congress was exempted from every single provision of the Civil Rights Act.

As in all stories of lost innocence, this one includes the older, worldly wise adviser. Mine told me that this was no big deal. He said Congress routinely exempts itself from labor laws and other legislation providing basic decency.

I did not find comfort in this, as characters in such stories never do. This was the beginning of skepticism—not cynicism—about those who claim to lead us in Washington. This skepticism places on officeholders and office seekers alike the burden of proving that they are willing to live by the rules they make for others.

Over the intervening years, little has changed. I have not been surprised to find that Congress continues to exempt itself from its great and small reforms. Whenever I have addressed these concerns to an elected official, the answer has been what it also is to the question of meaningful campaign funding reform: the other party prevents reform. The fact rather seems to be that the Congress does not have the corporate will.

The Hebrew Scriptures criticize unprincipled government: from the prophet Samuel's warnings of what would come with kingship to Ezekiel's denunciation of "false shepherds" who cared for themselves and not the people.

Jesus focused this tradition with his criticism of those who held high office but were not servants of the people. He confronted directly those leaders who "bind heavy burdens but do not lift a finger" to help people bear them. Until Congress sends the people the signal that "we are in this together," politicians will remain the subject of jokes and laments.

Congress lacks moral authority not because of the failings of a drunken senator here or a lecherous representative there. It lacks moral authority in part because it refuses to be held to the standards it sets for others. It also has authority problems because its members, of either party, are beholden to the interests that put them into office, but that is another question.

In a democracy the ultimate responsibility for what the government does rests on the people. It is the obligation of those who hear the message of the prophets to insist that those who govern lead by their example and ready participation. When leaders take that attitude they take a major step in rebuilding their authority.

# Shall We Fund Education or Institutionalize Poverty and Racism?

A recent cartoon in *The National Catholic Reporter* caricatured a jubilant Uncle Sam. Frame one: "We're on top of the world." Frame two: "The stock market is booming. Unemployment barely exists. Budget deficits are a thing of the past." Frame three: "Money is pouring in. We're rich!" In the concluding frame Uncle Sam says, "Someday we might even be rich enough to educate our children."

My work takes me regularly to fourteen Pennsylvania counties. One thing that strikes me is how wonderful public education is in some areas and how desperately neglected it is in others.

In the few years I have occupied my present position, three cities in Pennsylvania that contain some of the worst schools have been willing to assume burdens up to a billion dollars for sports facilities. In one of our cities, schools are so underfunded that teachers buy basic classroom supplies with their own funds and local churches cooperate to raise money for textbooks. To educate our children is primarily the state's obligation, but also local government's. Nonetheless, children who most need the education ticket out of poverty are being deprived of it.

Our way of addressing educational issues in this state institutionalizes poverty. That so many of the children who are the victims of this situation are Hispanic or African American suggests that racism also is institutionalized.

Children have a unique role in our society. Though politicians often call children "our future," their needs are in the here and now. It is up to our state government to do what has been done in so many parts of America, making sure that educational resources are distributed adequately now, not in a few years.

One frequently hears of how difficult it is to get a good labor force in America. Does it not occur to anyone that the solution to that problem starts in grammar school? The teams and businesses that will profit from the events ought to be building the sports facilities. Dishonest trickle-down theory, suggesting that money eventually reaches those in need, sells the public on huge sports facilities. The truth is that many bites will have been taken out of the pie before Alex and Megan see their share.

Obviously we can't have it all without increasing taxation, so we have to learn to accept limits. This is perhaps the hardest thing for baby boomers to accept now that it is our time to run things. Although we have experienced what feels like wealth without end, resources are limited. If the topic is health, transportation, or education, we have to learn how to manage what is there without immediately asking for more.

The word from religious circles that has become business parlance and desperately needs to penetrate political circles is "stewardship." It's about distributing limited resources in a world of apparently infinite need according to accepted major goals. To adopt a stewardship view on a personal level is to ask how one plans to fund his or her life's main goals. We really are familiar with this kind of thinking. Do we spend money today for a pool in the backyard, or do we put that money away for retirement or a child's education?

Still, we assume that on the public level resources do not have to be managed in terms of goals rather than votes. We need to remain aware that there is an education crisis in Pennsylvania and remind ourselves that not everybody can have everything they want. Can we have both schools and arenas at the present level of taxation? That is a question for economic experts. If we must choose between stadium and school, however, let's choose our children and their future.

## Recapturing Public Moral Sense

Will Rogers complained in the 1930s that most people spend six days sowing wild oats—and one day praying for crop failure. Something in each of us wants cause and effect suspended, just in our case. We do not take proper care of our bodies on the groundless assumption that habits that kill others will leave us unscathed.

A generation ago, defying moral conventions was seen as brave and self-affirming. Cause and effect seem to be at work. There is a rudderless feel to much of American life today. There is a sense that people probably should get away with what they can and that questions of right and wrong are matters for individual choice. Have we abandoned the concept of public morality?

Actually, we have forgotten that laws do not have much claim on our obedience unless they reflect society's beliefs about right and wrong, or some sense of the nation's agreed-upon purpose. Our agreed-upon purpose, expressed in our Constitution, is "to establish justice, insure domestic tranquility, provide for the common defense, promote the general welfare, and secure the blessings of liberty to ourselves and our posterity."

These are moral concepts whose implications we are invited to work out in each generation. But who wants to think about, let alone debate, such slippery concepts as justice, tranquility, welfare, and liberty? What if we were forced to take up public discussion of these issues? Might we see that it is not true, after all, that "you can't legislate morality"? Might we see that in this constitutional sense, except for administrative regulations, we hardly legislate anything else?

We have also forgotten that the test of any civilization is the degree to which people obey its unenforceable laws. It matters that people choose not to get away with what they can. It matters that I see my integrity as contributing to the public welfare. There is a very public aspect to personal morality. Being a good citizen is about contributing to the public good through personal effort that begins with habits of mind, with the little things.

Lent, for most of the world's Christians, is a season of self-examination, change, and growth. The religious word for that is repentance. The annual Lenten season is a reminder of what should be a daily discipline. Looking inward and making adjustments is a necessary part of life. As we baby boomers age, as we have begun to take over the world, we may want to reconsider our understanding of the place of morality itself in private and public life.

We might start by admitting that "If it feels good, do it" has proven itself to be a recipe for disaster. Instant gratification has proven itself to be the real opiate of the people. Without bowing to the rhetoric of demagogues or religious extremists, we boomers need to say, yes, there are too many children growing up without two parents because some of us were irresponsible. Yes, there are too many children growing up poor because their fathers pay very little or no child support. Yes, we did not let our children decide what vitamins and clothes and schools they needed—but we pretended it was up to them to choose a moral or religious code without our guidance or example.

Lent is a great time to start thinking in a disciplined way about what our values are and how we can reconnect them to their sources so they can become more fully a part of us. Lent is a time to consider how our values, undeveloped as they may be, must inform our lives in the small things so we can help with society's big issues.

## Casinos: My Money Is on the Moral Questions

I'm not opposed to gambling as an amusement. I occasionally buy a lottery ticket, and I permit raffles in the churches under my jurisdiction.

When I recently expressed concerns about casinos in the south side of Bethlehem, where I spend most of my time and have some understanding of the neighborhood, the knee-jerk response from a real estate investor was, "Bishop, you can't impose your religious beliefs on others."

Besides noting the sleaziness of poisoning the well of discourse with decayed red herrings, I want to make two points.

The first is Democracy 101. In our system the state may not set up an official religion. I'm for that. My own religious group was relentlessly persecuted with state connivance for more than a century in Connecticut and other parts of New England. Nonetheless, nothing in our system prevents anyone from arguing for their principles, whether those principles come from ancient texts, gold tablets in Elmira, Chairman Mao, or Adam Smith.

Although I do not share the position of the majority of religious people in the United States when it comes to reproduction and sexuality, I would not wish to live in a country where their voices were stifled. I do not like our country's leadership to be enmeshed with the religious right, but they are allowed to be and I have to live with that.

Second, serious questions that raise moral issues remain to be asked about proposals for slots parlors on the south side of my town. Answering them is imperative for anyone whose moral sensibility is located this side of Pennsylvania's great Robber Barons of the 1800s.

What happens to the neighborhoods of the relatively defenseless blue collar or poor citizens? Should columnists, politicians, and investors be the loudest voices in making decisions about neighborhoods they do not inhabit? Atlantic City has been dismissed from discussion with blithe promises that those mistakes will not be repeated and that this situation is different. Do we not have the right to see the numbers and read the contracts?

Why does the first big chunk of money go to Harrisburg, not the city that must provide the services? Will ten million dollars even cover the cost of services incurred by the city? (Research the economics of the gambling industry. Ten million is a fly speck on their balance sheets.)

These are moral questions.

Social services, especially those not funded by taxes, will surely be stretched. The operators of two soup kitchens assure me that they will have to close in the face of the load that casinos will bring. The ability to feed the hungry is a moral question for people of every or no religious persuasion.

Is the whole truth being told about touted new jobs? Has the gambling industry ever hired local people in great numbers for more than relatively menial jobs? Show us the written commitments to train and hire south side residents for the significant jobs.

Should Northeast Pennsylvania once again be raped by outside interests as it was during much of its mining history? The owners and other principal investors in the proposed gambling parlors live far away. Can we reasonably expect them to commit to a community in the way the former occupants of the site did?

Would less harm be done by locating a gambling center—and the trade in drugs and sex that nobody seriously denies it will bring—away from a neighborhood and its children? There are other places in Northampton County that would be easier to get to and much more insulated from neighborhoods that include families.

It is legitimate to ask whether the motives of ambitious young politicians have been scrutinized. The peril of small cities is that they often serve as stepping-stones for those hoping for more in their careers. We have a right to some assurance that no thralldom to the governor's wishes clouds anyone's objectivity.

Aren't these all moral questions? It may well be that they can be answered, perhaps splendidly, by the advocates of the south side gambling project. Those answers will never be forthcoming, however, if questions cannot be asked also by people who happen to believe in God.

# CHAPTER FIVE
## Preaching to the Choir—Church Life

### Does Your Church Fill All Mugs?

My friend Bob loves coffee. He also drives a lot. Like many people who share those traits, he has collected a variety of mugs that fit in his car. He starts the day with a clean mug and stops at various coffee sellers to have it refilled as his day goes on. The refillable coffee mug is a convenience all around: Bob has a cup with insulation and a handle, the coffee vendor saves the cost of the paper cup, and the environment is spared further strain. For years this daily pattern has gone smoothly from the first jolt of caffeine in the morning to the more soothing blends of coffee taken in the afternoon and evening.

Until last week. A young man in a high-end coffee place where he often gets his mug filled decided that because Bob's mug that day was from a donut store it was not worthy of this particular coffee chain, and so refused to fill the mug. Being a calm and gentle man, Bob simply ordered a large cup of coffee, and as the young man rang it up, poured it into his mug. I'd love to say that he left the empty paper cup on the counter, but Bob is also considerate of those around him and did not leave a mess.

As I consider the other ways this scene could have played out, especially if a less calm person had been there, I admire Bob's behavior very much. He wanted the coffee and did what it took to get it without starting a fight.

Religious groups exist in part because they believe they have something valuable to give the world. Time after time, however, sociological studies indicate that religious people are very hesitant, on a local congregational level, to share with people who are different, whose mugs may come from the wrong shop, so to speak. Race, economics, class, and other distinctions work themselves out in many ways, some quite subtle. Fine points of theology can be magnified to become litmus tests that simply reinforce the group's need to be by itself and not have to contend with what challenges the group's illusion of certainty and stability.

Nonetheless, Bob's approach can work. A woman named Lorraine recently said to me of her church, "Everyone was very nice to me to me on the surface, but it was four years before anyone took me seriously as a person." She had simply been persistent because "she wanted the coffee," so to speak, and decided to outlive the congregation's resistance to a new and different person. Like Bob, Lorraine decided that confrontation was not the answer in her case. Where Bob *outsmarted* the clerk, Lorraine *outlasted* the exclusionary tendencies of the congregation.

Bob and Lorraine were whole enough to take care of themselves well and get what they needed. Whether we are trying to sell their brand of coffee or promote a religion, we must realize that people will appear with mugs that may be different. The hard question for religious communities is whether they are willing to fill whatever mugs are brought to them. Had the young man in the coffee shop been a little less afraid of what was different, he would have kept a customer. Many congregations complain about "revolving door syndrome." They have lots of visitors and consider themselves very friendly, but nobody stays. When churches undertake the discipline of learning about the ways they unconsciously exclude, the ways that power is just as unconsciously kept in small circles, they may find that the doors have stopped revolving. Imagine your place of worship with a sign saying, "We'll fill your cup, no matter where you bought it."

---

## On Daily Hunger

"Give us this day our daily bread." The familiar phrase in the Lord's Prayer may most accurately be translated, "Give us today one day's worth of food." Like the rest of the prayer, it is something of a challenge, and shows us the distance Jesus perceived between his followers and the comfortable people.

The prayer is not the prayer of the fat cat, the arrogant, the complacent. It puts all who pray it in the same place as the Israelites who could take only one day's worth of manna in the wilderness: we must trust God again tomorrow. In this scenario, he who dies with the most toys was playing the wrong game.

If you know anyone who has recovered from addiction, you know that one of this person's spiritual survival techniques is to get through "one day at a time," which some parishioners have reported to me actually means one hour or even one minute at a time. They tend to report that they get what they need, but not a lot more, because complacency is their greatest spiritual danger.

Uncomfortable as it may be, it is an experience of grace to get by on just enough food or faith to live through the present moment. It is a gift of great value to know that one's hands are empty—deliverance from complacency and arrogance is no small gift.

The most frightening thing about this phrase in the Lord's Prayer is that it really does mean that the spiritual quest involves yearning, the sense of not having. "Thy kingdom come" is the plea of those who know it is not here yet. "Thy will be done" makes sense only to those who see how much it is not yet done. "Give us this day our daily bread" is the cry of those who do not have more than they need.

Nobody likes to think of themselves as poor, as lacking. Therefore most of us blunt that side of the religious message, using religion to assure us of what we have, of permanence, of control. Jesus works against that in these few shorts breaths of prayer: those who pray his words are forced to focus on how much they do not have, how temporary they are, and how much there is to do in the world.

Put another way, those who "hunger and thirst for righteousness" have something to look forward to, are people God can work with. Those who think they have or know it all are just in the way.

In this sense, the awareness of want is a gift. Those who do not think they have all the answers can learn. Those who sense their own incompleteness can grow. Those who are looking for something make the discoveries.

The greatest violence done to Jesus was not the cross, horrible as that was. The greatest violence done to Jesus is the work of those who twist his message into support for the status quo, those who have made a nice guy out of one of history's most consistently irritating figures. That violence keeps his message from getting through.

In teaching his disciples to yearn, to acknowledge their hunger, he was preserving them from greed and keeping them available for growth.

The problem with everything I have said here is that it embraces rather than avoids discomfort. The polite put-down in our culture is, "I'm not comfortable with that." We are not here to seek the comfortable thing, but the right thing. They are seldom the same. When I want to tell Jesus that his recommendation of hunger and yearning is uncomfortable for me, I hear him say, "Good."

## In Praise of Name Tags

I feel naked. Sitting at an international bishops' meeting, I find that I left my name tag in my room. It's embarrassing. It feels rude.

This is a change for me. I once hated name tags. They seemed invasive and, well, tacky. Increasingly, however, parish churches have name tags both for regular members and for visitors. They help my work when I visit parishes: people are touched more directly when addressed by name.

As an "introverted sensor," I store up impressions and memories of interactions with each person I meet. Though my brain seldom has a name as the primary way of identifying people, I never forget faces and interactions. The data bit for the name gets filled last and requires some repetition.

This is frustrating in my line of work. Add to that the slightly neurotic fear of getting somebody's name wrong. Being in three or four different churches each week, then, can be stressful. I have learned all of the ways of speaking to someone cordially without saying the name. I cannot believe, however, that anybody is fooled.

When I arrive at a church that uses name tags, my breathing becomes easier. Even at diocesan meetings where I am the identified leader, I wear a tag to encourage the practice.

We like to know people's names. In turn, people like to be called by name. In parts of Africa, even if you have just been introduced by name, you begin your talk by saying your name—so that the hearer can say it back. Naming one's self and hearing listeners repeat one's name creates friendly space in which discourse is truly communal. Conversation and community begin in mutual recognition.

Knowing and being known by name is a mark of community in our culture. As churches grow, the tags help people to remember the importance of identity. I was ambivalent about the TV series *Cheers*, but I loved the title song about a place "where everybody knows your name." To a name forgetter whose own countenance is not particularly memorable, that sounds a bit like heaven.

The Hebrew and Christian Scriptures are rich with references to naming, knowing by name, and being known by name. Jesus knows his sheep by name. They recognize his voice. Christians are never baptized as groups, but as individuals and by their first names. Life can deprive me of a great deal; in relationship to Christ, however, I always have a name.

I was walking with a friend on the streets of Allentown, Pennsylvania. A homeless person approached us. A kind of rant began, a mixture of desperation and need with an edge that might frighten some.

At the first pause, my friend interjected, "I'm Father X; what's your name?" Everything changed. Tempo, volume, and tension in the conversation gentled, and we were able to be of some help to that person.

A street minister in South Bethlehem makes a big part of his ministry simply knowing people in the neighborhood and saying a few words in their language. People feel differently about themselves and their lives when someone who does not have to do it cares about their identity.

Everybody is going to have different skills at remembering names. We can probably all work a bit harder at it. In the meantime, name tags will help. Whatever our skills in that department, however, expressing interest in who people are is something each of us can do. It is part of the shepherd Jesus' insight that belonging often precedes believing.

## What I Have Learned from Women Clergy

In 1976, the Episcopal Church changed its canons to permit the ordination of women to all orders of ministry. Women priests and deacons are a fact of church life in ninety-seven of our hundred dioceses. In several, women are bishops.

In my Long Island parish I had two women associates. Several more worked with me in my New Haven days. Since coming here I have benefited from the presence and counsel of many women colleagues. I am grateful for the presence of women as colleagues in the ordained ministry. I reflect on what I have witnessed, on how ordained women have enriched my experience of Christ.

The center of Christian faith is the passage of Jesus through suffering and death to the life that gives us life. Christians are called to live that "paschal mystery," to offer ourselves for the sake of others. Often, that entails suffering. Always, it means God gives life to someone through our participation in Christ's self-giving.

The women clergy who have touched me deeply have endured open hostility, casual snideness, and patronizing behavior that perhaps comes more from ignorance than ill will.

I marveled at how my parish colleagues in Long Island were too focused on caring for God's people, much too thankful to God that their vocation had been realized, to spend a lot of time complaining. That got my attention.

Like Peter cutting off Malchus's ear, I fantasize about smiting those who use the word "priestess" with all its demeaning psychosexual implications, but this would help nothing. The women I admire have not been wimps or victim types, and do not need me to fight their battles. They have pointed out injustice, educated the church, and remained people of good will toward those who mistreat them. Certainly there are angry women and there are angry or even threatened men, but the vast majority of women priests have taken on this extra ministry of self-giving with holy equanimity.

Watching the reception of women clergy in the Episcopal Church USA has also deepened my belief in the incarnation—not as a long-past event, but as God's everyday method for conversion. People who, like most of us, are resistant to change, get hung up on arguing imponderables, bogged down in debates where either point of view can be sustained with piles of data. People who have found themselves effectively ministered to by women clergy, however, also have seen their fears and suspicions vanish like vapors. They could not remember what the fuss was about.

The anthropologists' conclusion that men fear women is not arguable, although it is not always remembered. How much this cultural factor has influenced theological discussion will be for future scholars to decide after the embers of debate have cooled.

In the meantime, I can say that for many men the experience of women as leaders, pastors, and authorities has been redemptive of that fear that so cripples human community. I do not have to ask myself whether women *can* exercise spiritual authority in the church in a way that brings health: I have seen it.

Receiving the ministry of women clergy in sacramental celebrations has expanded my awareness of God's generosity. We are only beginning to appropriate the riches of women's experience, only beginning to hear their report, yet the very sight of them presiding at the altar is the forceful reminder to me that attending to that other half of the history of salvation is vastly more delight than duty. As our theology digests the rest of the story, the world will be enriched.

## The Da Vinci Opportunity

There is no such thing as bad publicity. The furor over *The Da Vinci Code* is the religious right's gift to Hollywood. This kind of reaction gave the high-brow *Last Temptation of Christ* a popular audience: what it will do for a best-selling thriller cannot be estimated.

Let's clear the deck: yes, Hollywood has been offending Christians since Joan Crawford's *Susan and God* (1940) in ways it has never focused on Islam, Buddhism, or Judaism. Yes, for a historical novel, Brown's work is ludicrously researched and full of factual mistakes that make the suspension of disbelief needed for reading fiction almost impossible. Yes, Jesus' celibacy is easy to demonstrate. Yes, it is utterly improbable that a beautiful woman whose grandfather has been grotesquely murdered would go to bed with a middle-aged man with bad clothes sense just a few days later, although, as a male, I am somewhat willing to believe that one. And so on.

Pointing out the endless "errors" of the *Code* misses the point and misuses this godsend of publicity for the Church.

The real question is: why is the book, and presumably the movie, such a hit? As I travel the fourteen counties in my diocese, I have heard two themes from Brown's fans.

The first is that the *Code* resonates with the belief that religious institutions have occasionally been dishonest, manipulative, and very, very rich with no accountability. There is no major religion without blood on its hands, as anyone except the unlearned or the most defensive zealots will admit.

The second and even more common response is from those women who feel themselves to have gotten a very dirty deal from the big three "religions of the book," and it is certainly hard to disagree.

One woman said to me of Brown's book, "This is the first time I've felt that religion could affirm me as a woman." It would be easy to say that she should get out more, but it is more useful to say that Brown's fiction has evoked a response that more polished religious thinking has just plain failed to get.

For Christians to take a defensive attitude toward what is, after all, a book/movie that will never be considered a timeless classic is self-defeating. The reactive stance of some of my fellow believers suggests that they learned nothing from Islam's public relations disaster over *The Satanic Verses*. The reactivity of some Muslim clerics unfortunately confirmed every stereotype that many already believe about Islam. Do Christians now wish to confirm Brown's suggestion that the Church is defensive, secretive, and tolerant of violence?

If Brown is wrong in his indictment of Christianity, would it not make more sense to seize the moment when people are excited about a topic and invite them to experience the alternative reality?

Why not take the opportunity to invite people to experience institutions and structures that are transparent and accountable? Why not invite them to come to see how the feminine in all of us, and in women in particular, is honored?

If I had the money I would stand outside of theaters distributing copies of Marcus Borg's *The God We Never Knew* to offer just such an alternative view of the Christian message. As one writer has said of the *Code*, "We have our work cut out for us." Why not just do it?

To the extent that Brown is right about the nature of institutions and the rejection of the feminine, perhaps the best thing to do would be to change, and to do so publicly.

## Son of Encouragement

Does your stomach sink when someone looks at you seriously and says, "Now, I'm telling you this because I care about you"? Mine does, because often the speaker reports that an unspecified number of unnamed "people" have a gripe. Sometimes the speaker passes it on to whip you into shape—without saying what they themselves think. There is no grace in such a situation.

Everybody wants to be liked; everybody wants the approval of others. It is impossible to have both all of the time, but that is a hard truth to internalize. Is there an alternative to messy confrontations? Is there a way to get people to change that does not involve doing them psychic or spiritual damage?

The biblical authors stop every now and then to tell us what certain people's names mean in their native language. One such name is that of St. Paul's occasional partner, Barnabas. We are told that his name means "The Encourager" (literally, "son of encouragement").

Why bother to tell us that? I think the writer wants us to recognize that, in secular or religious settings, we do not employ encouragement as our primary tool for effecting change. We are good at setting out high ideals and urging people to strive for them. We are especially good at analyzing people's mistakes. Unaccountably, religious people often act shocked when they discover sin in their midst.

The result of a demanding and punitive moral atmosphere is depression and hypocrisy, not the desired behavior. Being a "Barnabas" is about effecting change by reinforcing the good that people do. This is especially important when they cannot recognize it, or it is an aspect of their character that is just starting to grow.

A book has been written about a remarkably successful teacher who grew up in Detroit. She went into teaching determined to make a difference in the lives of young people who had very little hope.

On her first day of class, she asked a nine-year-old with persistently bad language grades how to spell "cat." K-E-T was the answer the teacher received—delivered in the flat voice of those who have come to expect nothing of life. The child certainly did not expect the response she got from the teacher. "Mary, you're amazing! It's the first day of school, and you got one letter out of three right! I bet by next week you'll get two right."

Eventually the child did learn to spell, because for the first time in her academic life she had heard an encouraging word, a word followed by many more such words. She had been encouraged to think of herself as someone who could perform. Eventually she did. This story was repeated in that classroom thousands of times.

I do not believe that deciding to be a "son or daughter of encouragement" is simply the psychological fad of the week. It has to do with spiritual transformation. Throughout the Bible is the claim that redemption, however termed, involves a new understanding of oneself as part of those people through whom God does good things.

Whether or not one accepts the religious perspective on encouragement as a means of helping others—or ourselves—to grow, it is worth a trial. Choose a person who is struggling with some aspect of life. Encourage in this individual's behavior the tiniest hints of what this person might become. For instance, "You know, John, it's great that you let all the participants at the meeting speak their mind."

To help people recognize their potential, you might move on to random acts of encouragement in civic or religious organizations, in stores, or at home. The question may well turn out to be whether the encourager or the person encouraged will change faster. That's the beauty of it.

## There Must Be Boundaries in Churches

Are wars started by the nice guys? In his breathtaking *On the Origins of War*, Yale's Donald Kagan explains why he thinks they are. Examining evidence from ancient Greece through the 1962 Cuban missile crisis, Kagan observes how pride, honor, and other psychological aspects of nationhood play at least as much a role in the spawning of war as do territorial and economic needs.

Kagan concludes that those who appease bullies pave the way for war. Those willing both to take clear stands and back them up preserve peace. Our psychologist friends talk about the ability to draw clear boundaries. Kagan's theory about war and peacekeeping is as politically incorrect a theory as one can have in our time. It does not sound like the much-misunderstood "turning the other cheek" or the unwritten eleventh commandment, "Be nice."

Neville Chamberlain encouraged Hitler, whereas John Kennedy's tough stand forced the Soviets to pull their missiles out of Cuba. There may be something worth considering here, even if Kagan's prescription does not sound like what a really nice person might say.

Perhaps the clearest wisdom is contained in the phrase, "Never again!" It puts the world on notice. The determination of the Jews to be blunt about not allowing themselves to be victims is wisdom won through millennia of bitter experience. All too often, nice guys simply do not finish at all.

It was once my inexpressibly sad duty to shut down a church. There were several reasons for this painful decision. What seemed utterly unfixable was an ingrained pattern of conflict that caused the church to be known in its community as "the fighting church." It was the hardest thing I have had to do in my life and it was a costly decision for me. Still, a line had to be drawn: a church that harms people and will not see that it does so cannot be permitted to continue the harm.

I do not know about synagogues and mosques, but I do agree with the observation that people get away with behavior in church communities that would not be tolerated anywhere else. The core values behind this dysfunction seem to be precisely those Kagan finds behind war between nations: pride and a distorted sense of honor or worth. There is nothing people cherish so much as a perceived insult or hurt.

Can churches be healthy enough to say to actively or passively aggressive bullies, "Change your behavior or you may not be a part of this community"? It is an idea found throughout the Bible, in the words of Jesus and the writings of the apostles.

There is such a thing as intolerable behavior. When members of a church community denigrate or attempt to control each other, a boundary must be drawn. For their own sake as well as that of the community. Every person who says "If the church does this I'll never contribute another cent" must be told we will find a way to get by. Every person who says "If this happens I'll quit the church" must be told we will miss them. Every person who says the truth hurts their feelings must be told to get over it. People who refuse to "be in love and charity with their neighbor," refuse to give up resentments, need to know they poison their own soul and defile Christ's cross.

Many doubt that religious institutions retain the backbone necessary to preserve their own existence. In a time with no social pressure in favor of church membership, we may find out if that doubt is well founded.

## Forgiven but Not Absolved

Your spouse cheated on you—and tells you about it. Under most traditional religious systems you have the right to a divorce. Perhaps they apologize. For whatever reason, you do not act on your rights. You choose not to cut them off. That is the basic Christian understanding of forgiveness: God's refusal to end a marred relationship. The gift is given, through the pain, because God values the relationship.

Your marriage goes on, but you notice you are not interested in intimacy and your trust level may be quite low. Your erring spouse has to recognize something: they have been forgiven for violating the relationship between you, but they have not been absolved of the consequences of their action. It may come as a shock to the forgiven to know they are not necessarily absolved. Profound healing may entail considerable suffering.

Christians understand Jesus to have fulfilled the prophet Jeremiah's promise of a new covenant based on the forgiveness of sins. We hear the words, "This is my blood of the new covenant, which is shed for you and for many for the forgiveness of sins," each time we celebrate the Eucharist. Because forgiveness is a key Christian understanding, we sometimes oversimplify the notion for others and in our own minds.

Early Christians generally came to say that forgiveness means something when there is a change of heart, restitution whenever that is possible, determination to change behavior, and perhaps a period of penitence to allow change to take place. St. Paul was serious when he advised his readers to "work out" their salvation "with fear and trembling."

With our married couple, something more than giving up vengeance is required if their emotional life is ever to regain what it lost. The process beyond forgiveness, that of reconciliation, takes time, energy, and tears—if successful, it leads to deeper levels of forgiveness and reunion.

In life, those who love us forgive us for much of which we are not even aware. Those offenses of which we are aware, however, call for action on our part, not to earn forgiveness but to implement it through change, growth, and reconciliation.

To "come to Jesus," as the saying goes, is the beginning of a journey, not its end. The invitation to Christian life is not a get-out-of-jail-free card. This thought is not owned by us who do not identify as Protestants. The very first of Martin Luther's famous "Ninety-Five Theses" was that Christ calls people to entire lives of repentance. Luther's emphasis on free grace was paradoxically an attempt to make the converted life more serious.

Most conflicts I see in church and in ordinary affairs require less forgiveness and more reconciliation, less denial of pain and more exploration of problems and attitudes. Reconciliation between individuals or among peoples requires the work of understanding each other, of working through history that is often painful, and of constructing a way to live where all are respected and their rights acknowledged.

The South African determination to avoid a reign of terror by requiring former oppressors simply to tell the whole truth about Apartheid was an important example of how healing begins. Not with the cheap grace of "let's forget about it." To forget some things may well take centuries. Because the South Africans have painfully owned what has happened among them they are in a position to rebuild their society, even though that is proving to be a long and complicated project.

Care about using words like forgiveness and reconciliation can deliver us from quick fixes that do not work, and lead us to deeper and more lasting healing of our relationships with God and each other.

## God Changed the Retirement Age Before Social Security Did

Three travelers come to the home of the childless couple Abraham and Sarah (Genesis 18). In keeping with the standards of hospitality of the time and place, where the duty to protect strangers was absolute, Abraham offers them shelter and food. As conversation goes on, the frequently asked question comes up. "Got any kids?" There were no children.

Years before, God had promised Abraham and Sarah many descendants. Abraham was to be the father of many nations, with offspring too numerous to count. Abraham was now in his nineties and Sarah in her eighties, as the Bible tells it. It looked to him like that question was settled.

The traveler's reply is startling. He says he will be back in a year and, by that time, a child will be born to the couple. Sarah, listening through the tent flap, laughs bitterly. She gets right to the point: "After my husband has grown old and I am old, shall I have pleasure?" If we take the story on its own terms, what is contemplated is remarkable biologically, psychologically, and aesthetically.

There was a dilemma. If God's promise to Sarah and Abraham was going to mean anything, they were going to have to overcome a hesitation that was certainly reasonable and attempt something they probably had not tried in years. The story in Genesis is that they got together and, from their act, God got a people started. Their child, Isaac, was named for the laughter—the joke was on them.

In times more recent than those of Abraham, a man in his eighties called a reluctant church to the Second Vatican Council—a council that shapes the lives of Roman Catholics and every mainline Protestant Christian today. Who would have expected that John XXIII, a genial old man seen by many as having been elected to be an interim caretaker, would open such windows? God, that's who.

The average age of active Christians is higher now than at any time. I suspect that would be true of other religious groups as well. Religious boomers and their parents are facing the realization that if their faith and values are going to be available to their grandchildren and great-grandchildren, they are going to have to get or stay busy in programs of evangelism and church growth. We are not all young, agile, or hip anymore, but there is nonetheless a call before us with an urgency that has not been felt since the revival period of the 1820s.

Most of us who read these words are not in our first youth, either. The reality, lived in our communities daily, is that God raised the retirement age long before Social Security did. We can still be agents of blessing to many if together we take creative action, trusting that when Jesus, now about two thousand years old, said, "I am with you always," he meant that for all people of all ages.

Ethel, a friend in her late seventies from Florida, recently wrote to my wife: "Ask Paul why the independent churches are growing and the traditional churches are not." My original answer was, "Because they really want to."

After thinking about Sarah's laughter behind the tent flap, I want to change that answer. "Because they believe they can and are willing to do what they have to do to get results." They are willing to address the culture as it is, and they do not wait for people to come to them. Will history remember the gray heads of our day as having met the crisis with extra effort, trusting God for the results?

## Religion after the Garage Roof

My son jumped off the roof of the garage, as has many a child, because he thought he could fly. More accurately, he did not know he *couldn't* fly.

Whether jumping off a garage, trying to make a bicycle fly, or getting a broken doll to come back to life, each child needs a story like this one. An important part of a child's development is learning about her limits, her difference from the world around her. It is amazing how important this learning of one's smallness is.

Until that moment, a child experiences total love and nurture from mother and the environment and assumes it's all hers. When she discovers her limits and imperfections a much more vital discovery can be made. Limited, imperfect, she finds that mother and father still love her, that she is infinitely valuable just as she is.

Healthy people grow up sensing themselves to be of infinite value. But if they stop there, they become truly dangerous. The final part of the process that begins on the garage roof is the discovery that every other person is of infinite value, too, and moves on to learning to honor the value in them even with their own limitations and imperfections fully present. That is growing up.

People who do not value themselves are not going to relate to others in the best way. People who do not discipline themselves to see the infinite value of the lives around them will also be threats. Loving neighbor and self makes sense only if the love of neighbor and of self is based on an awareness of the value of all life.

Whether you call those activities religion or spirituality, people engage in them in order to get a sense of well-being, a sense of order in the world, and a sense of meaning for their lives. They can help you grow up.

If one is a go-it-alone practitioner of spirituality, one has always to ask oneself if one's spiritual practices lead one to value others infinitely and how one gets better at expressing that value so that the world becomes, as the saying goes, "a better place."

If one is a religious leader or a person who has any say about what goes on in a faith community, the task becomes harder. Certainly people need to grow in the knowledge of their worth through all the stages of life. They indeed need to be reminded of God's call to them. As human beings in a pattern of growth, they also need to recognize the value of others, not as potential converts but as people to be honored and served.

This often means inviting people out of their comfort zones. Unless there is disciplined engagement with others seen as valuable, however, religion becomes a kind of personal property. God is domesticated into a kind of utility that gives one an hour's peace on demand.

Having fallen from life's garage roof, a grown-up and healthy religion is not solely concerned with making people feel good about themselves, and certainly does not dabble in making them feel superior to others. It does not reinforce feelings of persecution and victimhood, but asks its adherents how they will put their awareness of their own value and purpose into practice as they encounter other, equally valuable people.

Is your spiritual or faith community helping you grow up? It might be interesting to keep track of the messages you receive from it in the next month in word, print, image, or act.

How many messages move you beyond valuing self to valuing others (as something other than potential converts)? How many messages encourage suspicion or mistrust of others? How many messages keep you focused on the past? How many messages encourage you to move into a creative future?

## Churches That Want to Grow, Sacrifice

Among the first missionaries to come to America were Moravians. They came to slaves in Georgia and the Carolinas. The slave owners, though, would not allow slaves to be baptized. To do so would be to recognize them as equals, so they denied Moravians access to the slaves. In order to reach the slaves, the missionaries sold themselves into slavery.

Think about that. They did whatever was necessary, at whatever personal cost, to bring words of hope to people who had no freedom. One stands in humble awe at such a story.

I can't imagine that these missionaries so surrendered themselves for a "cause" or a freeze-dried idea. I can imagine that they did it because of their perceived call to do the work of the gospel and because they meant to be reformed in the image of Jesus Christ.

Each of us and our churches continually need to be so reformed. That happens not by debate or argument, but only in our doing the work of the gospel.

As we increasingly commit ourselves to that work, the Church changes and grows. There are no private Christians. We are part of an organism, the body of Christ. We are formed by experience, by what we do as we let the Holy Spirit lead. Surely that doing involves speaking, and our testimony needs to be clear, but it is by understanding ourselves as being in mission that we come to rely on and experience the presence of God the Holy Spirit.

When Jesus said, "I am the way, the truth, and the life," he taught us that truth is not just an idea. In the long run, truth is a person: Jesus, living the wisdom of God, with and for all humanity. Knowing him sets us free. We can claim to be Jesus' followers when we commit ourselves to live out the truth that Jesus taught, the truth that Jesus lived, the truth that Jesus was.

We don't usually realize how annoying, threatening, infuriating Jesus was to the good, decent, and respectable people of his day, people like us, whether they were the supporters of the leading conservatives (the Sadducees) or aligned with the leading liberals (the Pharisees) or just trying to get along under Roman occupation. He was infuriating to the priests and theologians as well. If Jesus were to walk among us today, I suspect we'd ridicule him on a talk show. That's one of the ways we publicly execute people.

Jesus most dismayed, perplexed, and outraged the good people of his day by meeting on friendly terms with, and actually sharing meals with, the agents of foreign oppression, tax collectors like Matthew and Zacchaeus. Jesus outraged decency more in that he also met with people otherwise identified as sinners by even the enlightened and progressive minds of his day.

In one strand of the gospel tradition it is Jesus' befriending "bad" people that provoked plots to destroy him. But who among us could ask for a better epitaph than the charge contemptuously hurled at Jesus: "Look, this one receives sinners and eats with them." What would they have said about the Moravians and the slaves?

If churches want to thrive there really is not another way than that of Jesus and the slave missionaries. As we offer ourselves as living sacrifices for the sake of others, our churches will change. As we become who we are in Christ for the sake of the world, slaves will be freed. Somebody we are led to care about will be helped. God's purpose will be carried out. Who could ask for anything more?

# CHAPTER SIX
## Conversations with Others

## Should Christians Seek to Convert Jews?

Should Christians seek to convert Jews? The Southern Baptists have drawn attention to themselves with their aggressive program of evangelization directed at Jews. Nobody disputes anybody's constitutional right to preach to others, or on the other end, to spit when their name is mentioned. My concerns are not about rights but rightness. What was offensive to most Jews and many Christians was the program's focus on Jewish festivals and the appropriation of Jewish symbols in the effort to convert.

Christians who are perplexed by Jewish outrage need to imagine how it would feel to be themselves a religious minority and have to explain to their children a barrage of public messages harshly reinterpreting Christmas and Easter.

The theology around ongoing attempts to convert Jews is complex, particularly as Christianity springs from a Jewish matrix. In chapters nine through eleven of his Letter to the Romans, a passage that betrays his own frustration and confusion, St. Paul puts the brakes on Jewish mission; he says his business is Gentiles, and he leaves the fate of Jews to the will of God. To complicate the matter, parts of the New Testament read outside their first-century context sound stunningly anti-Jewish, and others cannot be explained in any context.

Christians who seek to convert everyone rely on the passage, "There is no other name under heaven whereby we must be saved" than the name of Jesus, but for me, the question cannot be theological until it is moral.

Suppose those who feel a mission to convert Jews are correct from a religious point of view. They still must account for the grievous sin against God and the Jews in the long history of oppression, abuse, and even murder that Christians committed, permitted, or failed to protest throughout the centuries.

From the standpoint of orthodox Christianity, that sin is a double one. The most obvious is doing evil to another human being. The more insidious sin is creation of a Jew-hating culture that dominated the West for so long, a cultural reality that makes it morally offensive to turn around and make nice in a supposed historical vacuum. It is not difficult to empathize with those sects of Judaism whose adherents resort to spitting when certain references to Christians arise.

Before even approaching the question of the "completeness" of Judaism, I conclude that contemporary Christianity possesses no moral right to proselytize Jews.

People remember, especially people who have survived persecution. On the other hand, some people who have not suffered much try to live as though the past were another country. This is usually a mistake. Just as it is irrelevant for white Americans to say that because they never owned slaves, they have no responsibility for the culture of racism in our land, Christians who claim to "love" Jews enough to want to proclaim the gospel to them need to think what a Jew might hear, feel, and remember when that "love" is expressed.

No matter how pure contemporary Christians believe their motives to be, they must remember that they are part of a religious culture that has left a dark stain on history. We cannot escape the past. Guilt may or may not be corporate, but it certainly is communal. In the wise words of the late Rabbi Abraham Joshua Heschel: "Above all, the prophets remind us of the moral state of a people: Few are guilty, but all are responsible."

If there actually is a mission to convert Jews, it needs to begin with an entire millennium of repentance, respect, and cooperation—the building of bridges. It would need to include intense and grateful listening to all that Judaism has to teach Christians. Perhaps, then, in the year 3000, there would exist a climate where the insights of Christianity could be shared (not shouted) in a genuine conversation that would provoke neither outrage nor bitter laughter.

## Is That the Bishop in the Dumpster?

(A story, especially for Lutherans, told by an Episcopal bishop, in 2003)

For many professions, there are some kinds of concentrated work that get done only if you come in early or stay late. Not being a morning person, I usually stay for a couple of hours after the office closes.

One morning I came in early to attack an unusually large pile of letters set aside the night before—they multiply in captivity. I experienced the desperate nauseated feeling that accompanies seeing a large empty space where something important should be. They say nature hates a vacuum, and I was not fond of this one. I went into panic search mode, repeatedly looking at all the places where the letters should or might be.

I have since read that psychologists have identified and studied this unproductive behavior of our species. Every time I find myself repeating it, I find little comfort in that fact, and I wonder what evolutionary purpose it would have served.

My older brother Mycroft once told me that when you have eliminated all the possible answers, it is time to work on the impossible ones. My worst fear, which was impossible, was that somehow my stack of letters had been dumped into the trash, taken to the dumpster, and hauled away. I couldn't remember which day the dumpster was emptied. There was a chance that it wasn't this morning. I went down to take a look.

Are you getting ahead of me? The dumpster, a big one, had been emptied the previous morning. There, on the bottom of the dumpster, was our trash from the night before. Among the bags of trash was the Amazon Books box in which I had stacked my letters.

On one end of the Cathedral parking lot on a busy street, our dumpster is a very public one. There I was in the somewhat conspicuous purple shirt that bishops in the Episcopal Church wear instead of a purple cassock. It was drive time in Bethlehem. Would I cause a major accident by hoisting my bulky frame into and out of a dumpster? If I waited for help, who knew what might have landed on my letters? Was middle-class upbringing right? Are people always watching?

Sometimes we cannot afford the luxury of neurotic paralysis, so I lurched and flopped my Nero Wolfe physique over and down into the dumpster. The letters were all there in the Amazon box.

With them safely in hand, I remembered Jesus describing the woman who turned the house upside down to find some money, and when she found it invited all the neighbors to celebrate. This was what I wanted to avoid. Rather, clutching the box, I rose deliberately to make my exit quickly. In midflop over the dumpster, I noticed three silver-haired parishioners standing by their car watching the apparition of the great plum.

I tell this story because this month our Lutheran brothers and sisters in their national assembly will consider modifying the Lutheran-Episcopal agreement of full communion. There is a good deal of resistance to that agreement in Pennsylvania, and much of it is based on a fear of overbearing bishops.

Perhaps, rather than getting caught up in endless theological arguments (unwinnable wars) and ancestral memories of Norwegian despots, those who worry can just hold the image of the dumpster-diving bishop of Bethlehem and try to live the relationship as agreed to and see what happens in God's time.

## The Christ Killer in My House

Images of Pope John Paul II at Jerusalem's Wailing Wall provided stark reminders of the long history of oppression, abuse, and even murder committed, permitted, or unprotested by Christians—our dark ecumenical stain on history, a grievous sin against God and the Jews.

Polish youths screamed at Jews headed for extermination that their suffering was vengeance for the killing of Christ. In this country, the Ku Klux Klan and other groups have justified their violence against Jews on similar grounds.

Mainstream Christianity, led by the example of Roman Catholicism, has worked to remove from thought and speech the idea that Jews are under God's wrath as "Christ Killers."

At the same time, there are writers who believe that the accounts in the New Testament of the trial and execution of Jesus are not accurate reports because the overall scenario the Gospels lay out would have been against the letter and spirit of the law at the time. This is odd, for from the trial of Socrates to that of Sacco and Vanzetti, from the Inquisition to the internment of Japanese Americans and the Hollywood blacklist, we know how laws are bent or ignored when convenient.

I don't find it useful to try to get behind the four Gospels. The ancient world did not understand the term "history" in the way we use it. Nor do I read the Bible to determine what it might say to or about others. Reading the stories of Jesus' betrayal, trial, and execution is moving for me because it exposes the Christ Killer in my house: me. If I want to pin the blame on anyone else, the story won't help me.

When I read of Peter's denial of Christ, I remember when I have not stood by friends because I feared social consequences. When I read of Jesus before religious leaders, I recall when I have chosen the good of an institution over the need for justice. When I read of Herod, I know when I wish religion to be a comfortable veneer. When I read of Pilate,

I know part of me concentrates on career issues. When I read of the fickleness of the crowd, I see myself in a culture that does not really know what it wants.

Briefly, when I read about the death of Jesus, I see business as usual. I see how the system works. I see myself; and I see you, gentle reader.

Why bother with these ugly reminders? The central teaching of the New Testament is that when human nature did its worst, God's love still pursued us. In the death of Jesus I see consistent love; in the resurrection I see love vindicated. To understand this story is to ask a question: When will the system stop doing its worst? This story exposes evil for what it is: cheap and relentless.

George Bernard Shaw's Saint Joan asks if each generation will kill another Christ. Even more penetrating: Will we ever learn to see around us the opportunities to stop the killing? We find token examples of evil corrected in each friend betrayed, each starving child, each victim of ethnic cleansing, every member of every dismissed minority.

Anyone who so understands Jesus' death realizes that the stories confront us with a life-or-death choice for daily living. Do my day-to-day words and acts bring death or life to this world? It is costly to give up business as usual, but it will stop the killing.

## Godless Orthodoxy and Holy Compassion

Shortly after September 11, 2001, area religious leaders gathered on the municipal plaza in Bethlehem. We are close enough to New York that most of us knew someone touched directly by the tragedy. Indeed, some area commuters had themselves been victims.

Among the religious leaders present were Muslims and Jews, both defying a stereotype, along with mainline Christians, including myself and the bishop of the Northeast Synod of the Evangelical Lutheran Church in America. We each tried to bring a word of hope or comfort, and a prayer.

With over two hundred million Americans grieving and frightened, we did what we could. We also witnessed to that fact that, while treasuring our own tradition, we shared the common ground of creatures turning to the Creator in a time of profound pain.

In the nation's largest city, at a ball park only a few miles from Ground Zero, a similar meeting took place, but with proportionately larger numbers and many more who were personally involved. Again, a wide spectrum of religious traditions were represented at Yankee Stadium in a ministry in a time of disaster. There was a Lutheran "bishop" (president) there as well. But things have become very different for him.

The Lutheran group to which the Rev. David Behnke belongs, the Missouri Synod, officially holds the view that for one of their clergy to pray with other kinds of Lutherans, let alone other Christians, not even or ever to mention Jews and Muslims, is a betrayal of Christ, and something entirely forbidden by one or two "proof-text" verses in the dustier corners of the Scriptures.

This man, who stopped on the way to Jericho, Long Island, to have compassion on a grieving multitude, may be defrocked.

Jesus was constantly in trouble for breaking the rules at precisely this point. He thought the Sabbath law must bend to human need (as other rabbis did and still do). He thought the compassionate Samaritan (an outsider of the worst sort) was worth a hundred religious leaders who failed to help the victim of a mugging. He sent cantankerous Saul of Tarsus to preach in both synagogue and pagan assemblies.

I hasten to add that many Missouri Synod Lutherans do not agree with the stand taken by the more rule-oriented among them. The head of the Synod is among them, as is an elderly lady who told me at a family picnic that "we are just so embarrassed" by the negative witness her fellow Missouri Synod members are giving.

They have no idea how petty they make the Christian message appear as they hound a man who was simply compassionate and respectful of members of other faiths who were themselves grieving.

Most of Behnke's persecutors are in the middle of the country. Some are in the Southwest. For them, 9/11 was something they saw on television. It is easy to be objective and play strictly by the rules when the subject is a two-dimensional image on a television screen. I say this not to accuse them of insensitivity, but perhaps to lessen the enormity of their sin.

I have come to call their attitude "godless orthodoxy." Whenever any of us thinks that the principles and systems are worth more than the people they serve, we commit godless orthodoxy. Rules and theological or philosophical systems have a great role to play. Without them, we would have to reinvent the wheel each morning. C. S. Lewis, however, asks the question, in *The Great Divorce*, that each of us must ask: Do I most love God or what I say about God?

I'm afraid that in the present situation God lost. How is God doing in your church's response to others this week?

# Mary the Mother of Jesus and . . .

This is a minority report. Virtually everyone agrees that Jesus was the son of a young woman named Miriam, Mary. Beyond that, agreement ceases. The overwhelming majority of Christians belonging to groups such as the Roman or Orthodox churches believe that Mary had only one child and remained a virgin throughout her life. Although nothing in the Bible supports it, there is a long tradition of such belief, and many of the most revered figures in Christian history have believed in this way. Included among them are not a few Protestants.

The minority view that comes to mind in Advent is held by those who believe that the conception of Jesus was indeed virginal. They honor his mother as "The God-bearer." They also believe that the Bible is to be taken at face value when it says that St. Joseph and the God-bearer did not enjoy a normal married life "until" she had given birth to the Messiah. This biblical statement seems to assume that they did enjoy such a life.

These believers take seriously the gospel report that Jesus had four brothers and two sisters (not cousins), and that his brother James was the first leader of the Jerusalem church. There is a very ancient inscription, in fact, that describes James as "the brother of God." The view that Jesus had brothers and sisters is held even by leading Roman Catholic biblical scholars of our day.

Is such a view of the essential normality of the marriage of Joseph and Mary, if it is historically true, helpful for Christian believers in any way? Perhaps it is.

It does remind us that married life is not a second-class kind of existence. The intimacy and the ecstasy of the marital bond are not "second prize" for those unable or unwilling to live without marriage.

Putting it another way, sex is not bad: the likelihood that the God-bearer enjoyed a normal married life reaffirms the idea that religion is to celebrate, not tolerate, the Creator's plan for humans to find joy and fulfillment in the union of heart, body, and mind that is marriage. What we cannot imagine Jesus' mother (or our own mothers) doing in her marriage we should probably also not do in ours—or else we need to look at our basic assumptions about marriage and sex very carefully.

Because women, tragically, must still continue to struggle for full status in our society, there is great strength to be found in the image of the woman who willingly undertook the most important task in human history without being asked to give up the other aspects of her life as the price of fulfilling her vocation and destiny.

The idea that Jesus grew up in an ordinary family gives a special depth to his story about the Prodigal Son's elder brother and his other stories based on family life and the relationships between parents and children. It gives a heart-rending quality to his proclamation that his "real" mother and siblings were those who followed him in faith, especially as he made this statement when his biological mother and family had come to silence him.

Those of us who invoke the prayers of the God-bearer both for each day and for the hour of our death do not call on one who was preserved from human existence, but one who lived it, full of grace.

Each of us is called to bear Christ in the world in some way, wherever and whoever we are. The possibility of the God-bearer being someone who by God's goodness walked faithfully and joyfully through life as wife and mother can call from us both hope and joy in God our savior.

## We Know Less than We Think about the Faith of Others

One of the most amazing parts of theological education for me was learning that the simplistic caricatures of Judaism, Islam, and Buddhism that I had learned in Sunday school and confirmation class were not just untrue, but wildly misleading.

In the decades since seminary I have continued to find remarkable the depth and profundity of those traditions. I have admired the variety of schools of thought within them. It is almost always wrong, I have discovered, to assume that all members of any group think one way, without nuance or variety.

Beyond that, I have blushed when communicators representing certain evangelical strands of Christian believing have crudely summarized some aspect of another religion's perspective in order to knock it down. I have quietly cheered when my fellow Christian leaders have been taken to task for unthinking remarks that show no awareness that, for instance, Jewish thought is as complex and varied as that of our own tradition.

I do not permit the churches under my jurisdiction to celebrate ersatz Passover Seders during Holy Week. Besides the insult to another tradition, such events assume that the Christians participating in them know things that they simply do not know about the rite they are aping.

Because I've inhabited that mindset for decades, it came as something of a shock to hear from Dr. Laura Schlessinger and again, during the recent holiday, from local religious writers who were trying to make an entirely valid point about their understanding of "forgiveness," just the kind of simplistic and dismissive caricature of Christianity that I had heard about other faiths in my own childhood. This is not the place to explain their errors—it is much more important to point out the universal problem: we all think we know more about other people than we actually do.

As distasteful as the experience of hearing Dr. Laura and reading the newspaper piece was, it was still helpful for me. My resolve never to try to speak with authority about a tradition in which I do not live has been strengthened.

It also left me with the wish that those who emphasize the importance of interfaith understanding would come to believe that such understanding must always go in both directions. Those who are part of what is wrongly thought to be a homogenous majority are the most likely to be stereotyped and misrepresented.

It seems to me that in the 1960s and 1970s both ecumenical and inter-faith dialogue came from an honest desire to understand each other better, to find how our common humanity is expressed in and built up by our spiritual traditions. Recently, however, we find ourselves taking increasingly defensive positions.

A recent teaching entitled *Liturgiam Authenticam* instructed Catholics that their translations of liturgical texts should no longer give the impression of commonality with those of other Christians, a sharp reversal of policy. Gone in a pen stroke were the decades of efforts in precisely the other direction. I'm sure there were strong reasons for such a change in position, but it leaves me just as stunned as did Dr. Laura.

Is there any way back to the virtuous curiosity and respectful dialogue we once knew? Is there any way back to a time when all groups had the humility to know that every other group was as complex as their own? That every other group operated with as much integrity as theirs did? A time when people sought commonality rather than divergence?

The third largest religious group in a recent survey (after Catholics and Baptists) is those with no religion (16 percent). Can the increasingly perceived irrelevance of religious faith motivate those who share faith to look for language that commends rather than belittles the faith that is in others? The question we are left with requires a courageous look within each of us: What keeps that from happening?

## Why Do Churches Exist?

Over the past few decades, a small industry has devoted itself to diagnosing mainline religion's "crisis." A focus on survival has ignored the original sense of crisis as a point of judgment—a point of evaluating performance and deciding identity and direction. When the institution appears to be in danger of disappearing, all but the most unthinking or insecure ask what the institution is for, and whether it has been effective in meeting its purpose.

One response to the crisis, as my own Episcopal Church has experienced it, troubles me. It is the idea that all will be well if we simply keep on doing what we do well, by which is generally meant emphasizing our talents for liturgy and the fostering of personal spirituality in the Benedictine tradition.

Readers from other denominations and faiths, I suspect, have heard the "keeping on" response in ways that apply to their own traditions. The suggestion that we simply keep on keeping on epitomizes the great American failure trap: if something does not work, do it more. More intensely. With greater fervor.

At its worst, the "do it more" syndrome assumes that the answers and the questions never change. The baby is kept in bathwater that may kill it, in a tub that stunts its growth.

There are ways to question this approach that do not detract from the importance of our traditions and gifts.

In opposition to the "do it more" fallacy lies the truth of the law of requisite variety: those who have the most options succeed. Those who face a crisis as a time to assess, learn, and attempt to change for the better are likely to make the helpful contribution. To use the law of requisite variety means being honest: learning from mistakes and wrong turns, learning to part with what has become obsolete.

Christianity's mission can be described generally as offering to people that fullness of life in God available to disciples of Jesus Christ and witnessing to Jesus' call for everyone to enact God's compassion and justice in the world. Our mission is to serve the world in the name of Christ, to extend compassionate arms even while new spears pierce Christ's body as they did on September 11, 2001.

The mission cannot be performed without intense self-awareness. Are we prepared to choose the right strategies for our time? If we are to perform the mission we have been given, we have got to be better at making explicit connections between people's lives as they are and the kind of life God offers in Christ.

Christian bodies have taken chances. That is a valuable trait. The value of the fact that American Christians have been forced by history to create an atmosphere where passionate disagreement is possible ought not be underestimated.

Experience suggests that those of us who preach will do better at helping the faithful to be faithful if we make more explicit and inviting the connection of the Church's activities to its identity in Jesus Christ, and if we do that in words and in ways that contemporary Christians can hear.

We live in an age when one risks being locked up as psychotic for claiming that God communicates; yet, in one way or another, that is what happens—at least when we learn to listen. Deep within us the Spirit breathes. We are invited to enter those depths. God heals us, gives us more than we can ask or imagine, and enables us to become agents of change in an unjust, painful, and starving world. Such transformation can be frightening—and life-giving.

# CHAPTER SEVEN
## Holidays and Holy Days

### Learning from the Revolution (July 4)

In my tradition, we have an obligation to observe Independence Day in church. It is, therefore, easy to forget that the American Revolution was opposed by many good Christians because the New Testament is clear about the duty owed to kings.

In Pennsylvania, many members of what would become the Episcopal Church and many Lutherans distinguished themselves in the Revolution. For even more of those people, the Revolution was a crisis of faith, and many of them did not participate. It rearranged their thinking not only about government but also about how God has ordered the world.

The Declaration of Independence is in part a theological document that claims that God is the author of human life and human rights, that governments get their power from The People, and that The People have the right to overthrow governments that do not appropriately provide for those rights. It reversed the traditional theology of divine right of kings deliberately and skillfully. For many Christians such an assertion flies in the face of passages by both St. Peter and St. Paul that command absolute loyalty and obedience to kings and emperors who, they believe, hold God's authority.

Had I been alive at the time, I believe I would have been as torn as many other Pennsylvanians, who realized that a message from the secular, somewhat "Deist" culture was asking me to change my thinking about God. I hope I would have made the radical change we now take for granted, two centuries later.

I have my doubts, however, about myself and about you who read this because it was not a lesson we learned once and were done with. Christians opposed the abolition of slavery, remarriage of divorced persons, votes for (or the ordination of) women, earning interest on money lent, life insurance, and even Social Security—all because of fairly clear passages or groups of passages in the Hebrew and Christian Scriptures that would need to be reinterpreted or quietly discarded.

These resistant people were not stupid or benighted, but they did base their thinking on the idea that things do not change, the idea that the Scriptures themselves do not show a variety of images of God and the *evolution* (let's at last embrace that word) of religious understanding. They also assumed that religion cannot and ought not learn from "the culture," much less from the spirit of the times.

But we do learn, all the time.

The assumption that religion must always be the judge and teacher of the culture and not also the student and beneficiary of culture seems strangely atheistic. It is, after all, quite scriptural to believe that "the spirit of the Lord fills the earth" and that nowhere and never is God "without witnesses," whether they know it or not.

At the same time, it is also true that Christians have put a unique stamp on some social movements, as the Reverend Martin Luther King's Southern Christian Leadership Conference or the work of Fathers Phillip and Daniel Berrigan may illustrate.

My basic beliefs are rather conventional, and I say the creeds without crossing my fingers. At the same time, I do not find any reason to believe that God's Spirit does not work in and through the lives of those who do not know or accept Christ.

Artists, poets, scientists are examples of those in whom I see the Spirit working—especially when they challenge or expand my awareness. My basic beliefs do not change because of their work, but the *implications* and the *applications* of those beliefs do change.

Even fundamentalists preach differently than they did a century ago because of what Freud began in Vienna. They have been taught by an atheist who sprang from another religious tradition. We do not need to resist this; we need to celebrate the multitude of our teachers.

Social movements, the arts and sciences, present opportunities for perception to grow. July's celebration of the Revolution is for religious people the reminder that "the world" is not necessarily the enemy, but may in fact be our teacher or, at the very least, may ask us important questions. Long live the Revolution.

## Our Debt to Coal Miners (Labor Day)

The coal mine tour guide's father died of black lung, and his grandfather died in a cave-in, so he had a particular authority. When he turned out the lights and showed us the amount of light a carbide lamp (and later a slightly brighter electric lamp) on a helmet provided, and added that this was all the light the miners had from the opening of the mine in the 1850s until its close in 1966, I began to realize what a different world they inhabited.

Long days mining an eighteen-inch seam on your belly; child labor starting at age seven; water, dirt, and noise; not to mention health, safety, and economic questions. A miner's life is not one I would have wanted. I understood why being sent to the mines in the ancient preindustrial world was a death sentence for a convict.

The industrial world we enjoy was built by the backbreaking labor of millions of people, supported by the unpaid labor of those who made what homes they could for them, with little hope for something better. We need to acknowledge our debt to them, not because they made some owners and investors wealthy (possibly some who read this today), but because they helped build a country, and for a long time provided much of the economic backbone of our region.

What have we learned? Our workplace is by and large safer and more rewarding than it was for those miners. Most of us have considerably more options about where and for whom we will work. Nonetheless, I think that the basic lessons still apply.

We are social creatures. Most of what we do and enjoy depends on what people do for us or with us. People are not to be used, but valued for who they are as God's creatures, and what they give to one another through their work. That gift is a continuing of the Creator's work. How do we teach that to our children so they will continue to build human respect and community?

We need to be clear in attitudes we model to our children, that while different kinds of work have different levels of responsibility, creativity, and reward, and while social conventions acknowledge this in many ways, everyone has the same personal worth. Our children need to hear us speaking of people from any walk of life with respect—whether they have more or less education, responsibility, or money than we.

Those of us who have shielded our children from doing volunteer work for the family or in community service may need to rethink that. How else will they learn that among those who follow Jesus, there are no little princes or princesses, but that we are members of one another? How else can they learn that the more privileges one has earned or inherited, the more responsibility one has?

Finally, work cannot be a god. Many species and some human groups simply kill or leave to starve those whose disabilities or age prevent them from contributing. We have learned to respect and care for them and to help them see that there are many ways to participate in the community's life.

Anyone who knows me knows that I am very far from being a socialist. My politics are independent and highly pragmatic, and I would never pretend to have expertise in labor relations. I am convinced, however, that if we believe that God made us, and made us to work together, we need to act as if that is true, and value one another accordingly. When that is happening, I am willing to trust the experts to do much of the rest.

## Holy, But Not Necessarily Nice (All Saints)

"I hear she wasn't a very nice person." Similar words greeted me with some regularity when I pointed out what a good thing it was that the Roman Catholic Church had put Mother Teresa on the fast track for the status of saint.

I have no personal knowledge of Mother Teresa, but my guess is that someone who gave her life to advocacy for the poor and got her hands dirty caring for the poorest might not be likable in the conventional sense, any more than Jesus was nice.

Something in our culture is willing to idolize recording stars and sports heroes but it rebels against the idea that there are heroes of virtue. We tend to express contempt when virtuous people make us fear that they think they are better than we are. How many young spiritual heroes have been squashed by well-meaning folks telling them not to be better than other people?

Mother Teresa practiced her game and developed her art, becoming a star in compassion and advocacy. It takes nothing away from us to recognize her focus and accomplishment. It takes nothing away from us to recognize her discipline and energy. It takes nothing away from us to contemplate the ways in which, in fact, she is better than we are. Or does it?

November brings to most Christians the question of sainthood—of heroism and holiness of life. None of the saints were perfect—the New Testament does not attempt to disguise this about Peter and Paul, and twice Jesus had to rebuke his mother.

Imperfect as they were, the saints revealed enough grace and virtue to be called "saints," a word meaning holy, that is, devoted to God. In each there was a flame that burned brightly for God and humanity.

Devoted to God: that is the major inconvenience presented by holy people, whether they are focused on the poor of the earth or transported in mystical contemplation. They are the people around us who are not in life for themselves, who have a cause from which they do not profit and from which they are not looking to retire in comfort. Builders of great institutions and communities or servants of the lowest, saints knew why they were alive.

When we think too long about holy people, we risk losing comfort with spiritual laziness. We Protestants say we know we are saved by God's grace. We are tempted to let it go at that, content with trying to stay out of trouble and occasionally helping a good cause. Contemplating the saints invites us to let God really make something of us.

Those of us who lift weights know that humans are all given the same number of muscles as a gift. What we do to develop them and keep them healthy is a matter of personal commitment, discipline, and focus. Gifts are to be used.

Unlike rock stars and sports heroes, each saint holds a record he or she hopes will be broken, and soon. The New Testament Letter to the Hebrews uses the image of the sports stadium, imagining the assembly of saints cheering us on, praying for us, encouraging us.

In a movie I like, Robin Williams plays a defrocked psychiatrist who tells a man struggling with smoking to find out whether he is a smoker or not, and then simply to be what he is. To think of the saints, each with their particular virtues, is to look deep inside for our own passion or focus, and to be what we are with a certain ruthlessness. There will be people who will react to that much focus by thinking we are not very nice: but that, after all, is a kind of applause.

## Shape the World with Two Words (Thanksgiving)

Inflation continues to strike. "Have a nice day" has been replaced at the checkout of my favorite convenience store with "Have a great day." This summer I even got "Have a terrific evening." The very prospect made me feel young, if only for a moment.

With all these good wishes coming my way, why do I miss "Thank you" so much? It would take fewer words, but that's not it. It has a host of socially acceptable responses without having to pronounce a similarly cloying benediction to "have a good/great/terrific day/evening" on the cashier. That's not it either.

Saying thank you is about acknowledging our interdependence. In a world where everyone feels entitled, it is a reminder that we are not entitled: we are dependent on the good will, efforts, and indeed, the cash, of others. In a society as complex as ours, nobody can go it alone. Oddly, the more prosperous one is, the more one depends on the efforts of others. No one is an island. No one is even a peninsula.

Even though I pay medical professionals or other service providers, I make it a point to thank them for their efforts. It reminds us that we are in this together.

There is more here, though, than even the health-giving qualities that saying thanks produce in those saying it by reminding them of their connectedness and interdependence. Being thanked also reminds the one who is thanked that each of us has a contribution to make to the welfare of others by how we expend our time, money, and energy.

People who sense themselves as interdependent are less likely to exploit or abuse their fellow citizens. A society that can perceive itself as interdependent is unlikely to tolerate the regal pretensions of those in government who are meant to be the people's servants. I dare to hope that if thank you was said often enough, democracy would be strengthened in America.

The rituals of ordinary life can reinforce this healthy attitude. The revival of saying grace at meals would not do anything to lower the incidence of food poisoning, but it would go a long way toward forming us as people who remember—whether we find the origin of our sustenance in the big bang or the six days of creation in Genesis or both—that our food comes from outside ourselves, and is also the product of the labor of many hands. We rely on a gift. When we recognize it as such, we might be more inclined to share it ungrudgingly.

For the overwhelming majority of the world's Christians, the central act of worship is the Eucharist, a Greek word for thanksgiving. In the Roman Mass, the Divine Liturgy of Byzantine worshipers, or the Holy Communion service of many Protestants, access to the central mystery of faith begins with a simple dialogue that includes, "Let us give thanks to the Lord our God." It moves on to words of profound thanksgiving. To the extent that they take this central act of their worship seriously, and let it move them, worshipers may find their attitudes transformed.

Whether we speak of religious ritual or the everyday rituals of saying thanks to all we rely on for income or services, thank you is a way to make us and our society more aware of our connectedness and our status as those who are recipients of what others have to offer. With that in our consciousness, celebrating the great day will take care of itself, no matter who wins the football game.

## A Time for Longing, Hope, Change (Advent)

Advent, the time before Christmas, speaks to us in many ways. I often find it helpful to think of it in terms of darkness, longing, and hope.

### Darkness

In the Northern Hemisphere, Advent comes as the world is darkening, as things appear to be dying. I am increasingly aware that someday Advent will arrive and I will not be here to greet it because I will be as dead. On the road to acceptance of one's mortality there are feelings of futility, of cynicism, of anger. My light shines so dimly; and the darkness, the afternoon darkness, the winter darkness, the last darkness, seem likely to overcome it.

So one old prayer for Advent began, "Stir up, we beseech Thee, Thy power, O Lord, and come." Advent is first and foremost about humanity in the darkness, longing for light to come, longing for God to act. Advent is permission, invitation, for each of us to enter the heart's fearful dark places that we try so hard to ignore most of the time, and to cry out, "Stir up your power, Lord, and come."

### Longing

To do that is to know something of the longing of God's ancient people, who knew bondage, who experienced exile, and whose prophet sang, "O that Thou wouldst rend the heavens and come." This time of the year is holy because we are asked to name in the very center of our hearts our common hope for humanity's survival and for its growth into a community of peace and equity.

With its memory of John the Baptizer Advent reminds us that longing is fine, that crying out for God is great, but that self-assessment and change need to be done to make room for Christ. For it is not God who keeps the fruits of the earth from reaching those who starve, it is not God who hoards power and wealth, it is not God who abandons spouse and children to scratch a midlife itch.

I remember then some more words of the first of those "stirrup" prayers. "Stir up, we beseech Thee, Thy power, O Lord, and come, that by Thy protection we may be rescued from the threatening perils of our sins."

"Threatening perils of our sins." Unless and until we understand that it is business as usual in the human community that defiles our life, unless and until we commit ourselves to change, to making straight in the desert a highway for God, there is very little that Christmas, that God, can do for us.

The unofficial fifth gospel, Charles Dickens's *A Christmas Carol*, reminds us that for change to happen, detailed memory and ruthless self-assessment need to come first. That asks us to work, work hard, for as Mary and Joseph knew, there is no easy road to Bethlehem.

### Hope

But Advent's preparation is not sustained penitence. The same ears that hear "make straight a highway for our God" also hear "Comfort, comfort my people, says the Lord." Advent is very much about hope.

Hope is the belief and the feeling that in the long run, life makes sense. Hope is what separates the believer from the cynic. The Scriptures teach that history, yours, mine, and humanity's, is going somewhere, and that history has the destiny of fulfillment in God.

Our sense of where history is going in God, our sense that in God our life has meaning, these are the foundation of hope. Hope is what generates a positive and productive attitude. When everything around appears to be a shambles, hope is what keeps us going, carrying on until victory comes.

In the coming of Christ, Christians see God's total commitment to humanity, the invitation to lift drooping spirits and intensify resolve to live the longed-for future in word and deed.

---

## Is Somebody Out There Having a Good Time? (Christmas)

Nobody thinks that Jesus of Nazareth was born on December 25. Why, then, is his birth celebrated on that day? The answers are simple—and revealing.

Winter is dark and also depressing. We even know a psychological condition called Seasonal Affective Disorder, appropriately abbreviated as SAD. Beyond depression, in days before electric light and central heating, winter also brought limitations on activity and threats to health. To rebel against such things through festivity and feasting is a natural part of being human.

In the Northern Hemisphere it was common to have celebrations in bleak midwinter, about the time that the worst darkness was past and the days began to grow ever-so-slightly longer. The breaking out of light in a time of darkness, a time when festivity contributed to survival, seemed an excellent time for Christians to focus on the birth of their light-bringer, Jesus.

The general festivity was there before the holy day. It is human nature and it makes good sense to engage in festivity in the midst of the cold and the dark. For this reason, it is not helpful for Christians to denounce any festivities in December or January because they aren't Christ centered.

There is, in fact, something hard-hearted about depriving people of a few moments' festivity in our stress-filled environment. H. L. Mencken once defined puritans as those who are obsessed with the fear that someone, somewhere, might be having a good time. Whether or not that is true, Christians do not help their witness by publicly wishing away the cakes and ale of others.

It is well worth remembering that Jesus' first miracle was at the wedding in Cana, where his contribution of water-into-wine is what kept the party going. The expression, "God rest ye merry," from the familiar carol, was a wish for the blessing of festivity.

If the ultimate goal of Christmas is to help us understand the incarnation, God's being with us in Christ, it should follow that Christians need to be with people, sincerely and evidently for them, if we expect them to credit readily the idea that God is with and for them.

On the institutional level, churches are with and for people through social and health-care agencies and in response to disasters and other special needs. What does being with and for people look like on the personal level? Only you know the answer to that. Each of us has dozens of choices to make daily.

When the greatest darkness comes and brings the cold with it, the hymn, "I Want to Walk as a Child of the Light—I Want to Follow Jesus," comes to mind. With it comes the question: What can each of us do so Christ's light shines?

Shine it does, and people do notice when we make the choice to follow. Recently Penn State gave its Beaver Award for Community Service to Dr. Randall Fegley, professor of history and political science at Penn

State's Berks Campus, and also a member of the Diocese of Bethlehem's World Mission Committee and leader in our diocesan initiative with the people of the Diocese of Kajo-Keji in the Episcopal Church of the Sudan. Randall's work for the Sudanese, a work that eventually involved many in this diocese, has been a witness to Christian commitment to bring light and joy to suffering people.

In wishing each of you joy at Christmas and peace and productivity in the coming year, I am wishing that in your merrymaking and in your quiet acts of service to others, the light of Christ will truly break forth and shine.

## Behind the Tinsel (Christmas)

Oscar Levant once said that if you look behind the phony tinsel of Hollywood, you will find . . . the real tinsel. I rather like a lot of tinsel on my Christmas tree, and will keep it. When I hold it aside, however, I see not more tinsel, but the challenge of Christmas.

It's a challenge of belief. I find a way to repeat each year the fact that Jesus did not ever, even once, *identify with* the poor. He *was* poor, all the time. There's quite a difference, the difference between interest and commitment. Similarly, Christians do not look at the manger at Christmas time and think of God's *identifying with* the human condition: they believe that God enters the world and shares our lot. Believing that is the challenge of Christmas.

I say "challenge" because the horrors of human evil are as real now as they were when Jesus was born. The mystery of disease, pain, and suffering also remains the greatest unsolved philosophical problem. In a world populated then as now with liars, cheaters, bullies, and bureaucrats, in a world where then as now the death rate is one each and there is plenty of suffering—in that world, Christians saw God appearing not as the vengeful warrior for whom some ancient sages had looked, but appearing vulnerable as one can be: as a baby, gently subverting the strong, the loud-mouthed, the manipulators, the arrogant, appearing in simplicity, totally dependent on those around him.

It is always something of a privilege to be invited to "hold the baby" when they are new and properly waterproofed. Holding and trying to communicate with a baby, perhaps hoping it will hang on to a finger, are times when we, too, enter a different, less-guarded, state. The point of telling infancy stories about the one who was to die bravely and mightily rise is to remind us that we are invited to a relationship with the divine that is never built on force. It is built on vulnerability, intimacy, and complete trust.

This is not to reduce the Christian religion to a club for innocuous ne'er-do-wells whose integrity is fulfilled only when they fail or someone uses them for a doormat. Intimacy, trust, and vulnerability take lots of work. Christians must engage what is amiss in our culture, and do so nonviolently. Vulnerability requires courage. The starving and under-educated children of the world need our constant care. Liking babies requires sacrifice.

The sacrifice is bearable because we know the rest of the story. As we watch the story begun at Christmas, it will reveal the living of unsentimental, faithful, and consistent love in the face of evil that is offered at Calvary and vindicated in Joseph's lovely garden. It is that sort of committed love that governments and individuals sometimes fear because it cannot be controlled and because it answers to a higher standard than expediency. It is the message on which tough guys, "real men," and "high-T" women heap scorn, because acknowledging it would expose the fear and anger that so often produces their aggression.

The news at Christmas is that in vulnerability there can be community. In trust can be found the power of God. In simple honesty with ourselves about ourselves, grace can flourish. In swallowing pride and accepting forgiveness from God or one another, a new creation can take place. When, in our Spirit-led imaginations, this child reaches up for us to hold it, we realize what Adam and Eve forgot for just one fatal moment: What God wants from us before all else is love. The rest will follow.

## In Swaddling Accessibility (Christmas)

It is the devil who wears Prada. At least figuratively. It's important at times to remember that. Each year I find a way to say that Jesus did not ever, even once, identify with the poor. He *was* poor. Joseph the carpenter earned less than what it cost to maintain an urban slave. Jesus would point out that he himself had "nowhere to lay his head."

Christians, with that in mind, do not look at the Christmas manger and think of God's identifying with the human condition: they believe that, in Christ, God enters the world and shares our lot. Jesus' choice to remain materially powerless for all of his life meant that the poor would not fear to approach him because they had no power or did not dress right. And those who did wear high fashion felt no competition with him and also approached freely. His clout came from the authority within him.

A messiah on Medicaid presents good news and a challenge. The good news is that the poor do not need to fear that life's circumstances put them outside of God's concern and acceptance. Poverty is not a mark of God's disfavor, as anyone who reads the Bible knows. Christian thinkers, most notably Roman Catholic thinkers in the last century, spoke in fact of God's bias in favor of those at the edges of life.

Those of us who are comfortable enough materially can also feel rejected or marginalized—just ask a chronically ill or a newly unemployed person or sit with a grieving person who feels nobody cares. The message of Christmas, that "God is with us," is most compelling when we feel abandoned.

The Christmas challenge to Christians individually and in our organized life is to ask whether we are as accessible as was Jesus to those most in need. I live in Pennsylvania's "Christmas City," and find it painfully ironic to contemplate how many powerful, name-brand, churches have left the inner city here and in neighboring towns for sprawling suburban campuses. They are happy to support charitable work in the city, quite generously at times, but the welcoming, available presence is just gone from the neighborhoods where it is needed most. I know the marketing concerns (and the overwhelming importance of parking) that can motivate abandoning the cities, but do wonder if churches who leave for the wide-open spaces consider conscientiously the vacuum they create.

Even to those churches who have elected to stay where the poor increasingly are, Christmas presents a challenge that brings me back to the title of Meryl Streep's delightful film, *The Devil Wears Prada*. Swaddling clothes are just rags. My strong personal preference is to show respect for people and for the sacred by dressing up. I have also come to realize in the last decade how the understandable desire that I and many others have to look our best when worshiping God may form a barrier to others' participation. I even have a few horror stories to share of people being made to feel unwelcome.

There may be mission potential in people with my sensitivities democratizing our level of dress-up for religious gatherings, just to make it clear that all are indeed welcome. Are they just as welcome at worship as they are at the church's food pantry or thrift shop? The first guests at Jesus' birth were the poor—farmhands tending sheep on the night shift. Would they be truly welcome to worship at the manger scene in your church, in mine? How we answer may tell the world what we think is going on at Christmas.

## Start the New Year Right: Ask a Question (New Year)

Most of us have started the New Year determined to be better people. Most of us recognize that there will not be peace or generosity for all until each of us becomes peaceful and generous—especially with people who are irritating or just different. Of the gifts God has given us for forming and maintaining relationships, the most underused is curiosity.

Think about how the typical fight between people begins. Person A makes some statement that irritates Person B, who then fires back an answer, often adding a put-down or hostile barb. At its worst, this kind of response indulges in mind reading: "You're saying that because you think . . ." or "You're just saying that because you're racist/sexist/anti-Semitic" and so on.

Then the real fighting begins. The subject originally brought up lies forgotten in the dust. If the people end up still speaking, all that remains of the interchange is a grudge. St. Paul spoke of a "dividing wall of hostility." There are few better ways to describe the results of verbal combat. A simple way to breach the wall is the disciplined practice of curiosity.

What if, the next time someone says something that angers or frightens us, or just seems too stupid for words, we use the sensation of being frightened or angered as a cue to defuse the situation?

Instead of simply repeating our own point (louder or more forcefully), what if we ask something like "How did you come to that conclusion?" or "Can you tell me why you think that?" Such a response opens windows instead of slamming doors. When we understand why a person thinks something, we may discover a new and possibly refreshing point of view. We might also learn something. At its best, such an approach opens a real conversation from which both parties can benefit.

It may take courage to try this when our habits (and adrenalin) suggest a more primitive response. It certainly takes self-monitoring and discipline to recognize and overcome our fighting reflexes. To our surprise, the discipline of curiosity may also enhance an experience with someone with whom we happen to agree. This column comes from reflection on a recent encounter of that kind.

I had arranged to meet with a fellow bishop who has taken a very clearly defined position on one of the issues that currently engages the Episcopal Church. I am trying to study and perhaps write about the issue. We talked over lunch and for a considerable time after that. When we were both sensing that the conversation was ending, he choked up a bit and thanked me. I was puzzled. I had gained from him a number of unique and thought-provoking insights. I asked why he should be thanking me.

He told me that, since he had taken this stand a few years ago, his fellow liberals had said nothing beyond congratulating him while conservatives had simply denounced his actions. I was the only one who asked how he reached this conclusion. He cherished the opportunity to explain his thinking.

I claim no virtue here: I wanted information for a practical use and did not consider the consequence of the interview for him. The entirely unintended consequence of my inquiry was that, for the first time, he felt that his thinking process and personal struggle were of value.

When our children say something that irritates us, especially if they might be right in their criticism, we tend to say, "Don't talk to me like that." How would a child's world change if we responded, "Why do you say that?" We could gain information and a child might begin to grow in attitudes of conversation rather than controversy.

Start the New Year right—ask a question.

---

## Messages for Latecomers at the Manger (Epiphany)

The camels have crossed our living room and made it to the manger. In our house, we toasted the three outsiders who made a perilous journey in hope. Their foreignness serves a point: *all* are welcome in Bethlehem. With the exception of those few Christians whose ancestors were Jews, the magi represent us as latecomers at the manger, outsiders.

A great deal in our culture—at school, work, and sometimes even at home—can make us feel like outsiders, like we don't amount to much, cannot contribute much. It can make us feel too old, too young, not respected, not useful. The first message of Epiphany, no matter what the world may say about you or to you, celebrates Jesus welcoming us at the manger, all we bring, and all we are. Nobody can take that away.

Epiphany's second message and meaning is about journey. To lay our eyes on Christ means to set out on a journey. Young or old, rich or poor, whoever each of us may be, to let God into our lives means that our lives are never the same again. We grow and change as we listen for the voice of the Spirit. It may look like home, but it's a new destination each day.

I hear challenges when I hear the story of the magi: Look for a star to follow. Look for a goal in life bigger than survival. Realize how much good you can do, how much of a person you can be for those around you. Dare to believe you can have a real and growing relationship with God.

Journeys have their good and bad points. The idea of always being on the road, always discovering the new, is exciting, sure, but it's also tiring. We traditionally depict the magi riding on camels: there is probably no more ill-tempered and uncomfortable beast of burden than a camel, but they were useful; because they were equipped for long journeys, people put up with them.

The sense of adventure also has a flip side of rootlessness, of disorientation. It is possible to believe in Christ, but hold back from letting God into much of our everyday lives. If you are like me, you would like to know as much as possible about where you are going, you would like to avoid making wrong turns—but without the indignity of stopping to ask for directions.

No matter what we may think about the value of the "institutional church," community in Christ is important for the journey. Because the journey can be hard, we come to the oasis, the gathering of God's people in the Church. A real oasis is more than a pit stop. The oasis was a place of safety, of refreshment, of sharing stories with other travelers, of trading tips and warnings about the hazards or changes in the trail.

For those who take their spiritual journey seriously, it is important to stay connected with the community that gathers around word and sacrament. The odds are against our surviving the trip unless we regularly come to where we are welcomed, refreshed, reminded of the directions, and just plain encouraged to keep at it.

Epiphany has a lovely complex of ideas: everybody is called, sent, and can be nourished along the way. It is our annual invitation to saddle up and risk the journey because we know who awaits us at its end.

## A Word to My Fellow Failures (January)

January is the pits for many people. Bills come in like sleet from December's generosity, and folks stare in despair at three dismal words: "minimum payment due." Once again, the promise to control finances was defeated by generous impulse and the high we get from shopping.

More painful is the experience of January 1 promises to ourselves that begin on January 2 to lie like corpses on a battlefield: the New Year's dieters who pick up that piece of fruitcake, the recent ex-smokers who find themselves puffing guiltily, the new joggers and walkers who find themselves glued to the couch. All suffer guilt and that strange phenomenon, the belief that if you slip once, the magic is over and you are free—obliged, almost—to return to the old behaviors.

The price of returning to old bad habits is a few recurring moments of guilt and perhaps a low-key sense of self-disrespect that some consider not a high price to pay for going back to what is familiar and comfortable.

But do January failures have a use beyond generating low-grade depression? Having had my share, I think that failure has several gifts to give.

The first is perspective. People cannot be defined by one or two character traits or habits. People are more than their waistline, bank statement, or golf game. Everyone has a different package of strengths and weaknesses. What is easy for one person may be difficult for the next.

When we think of ourselves do we think primarily of our assets or our deficits? The answer to that question can tell people a great deal about themselves, and about their religion.

St. Paul apparently had a physical or psychological defect that he could not overcome. Despite his repeated prayers, no cure was given him. Instead, he heard in part, "My grace is enough for you."

Our worth starts not with our relative perfection, but with God's love for us. "Amazing grace" boils down to the fact that life is a gift, not a task, and that the answer to failure is forgiveness and restoration.

Failures also remind us how susceptible we are to cultural signals, and how we are responsible for what goes into our brains. People struggling to overcome a bad temper or bad language who continue to watch "action" films are not making things easier for themselves. People with spending problems who continue to read every catalog that comes in the mail and subscribe to fashion magazines are asking for trouble.

Failures to pull ourselves up by our own bootstraps remind us that, for some things, getting help is the only answer. Human interdependence is a part of our nature that is often underemphasized, whether from pride, fear, or arrogance, I cannot say. The facts seem to be that certain kinds of behavior can be changed only with the help of professionals or support groups or both. Failure can teach us that seeking help is not defeat, but wisdom.

Not everything can be fixed by will power and a supportive environment. Many things that were considered moral failings a generation ago are recognized as medical problems today—and not all of them are easily treated, if they are treatable at all.

People who were once judged as lazy, weak willed, stupid, or daydreaming are now understood to have infirmities as real as a broken leg, but not as easy to treat. We are increasingly aware of the genetic basis or predisposition to a wide variety of behaviors.

Perhaps this information together with our own experience of failure in keeping New Year's resolutions can make us compassionate rather than judgmental when we encounter what seem to be the deficits of others.

## Groundhog Day, February 2

Would you like to get everything right in your life? Now that Punxsutawney Phil has made his promises, it may be safe to admit my long-standing fascination with the Bill Murray film, *Groundhog Day*, about a man who is given the opportunity not only to correct his failings but even to develop skills and talents. Murray's character changes from shallow prima donna and manipulator to a caring, reflective, and cultured man who plays a mean piano and risks his life to save those around him.

The gimmick is that Murray is given thousands of repetitions of the same day to get it right—to change and mature, even though he was not seeking that blessing. I would give anything for a Groundhog Day opportunity to stop the world, be purged and perfected, and then pick up my life exactly where I left it—and go on as saint, lover, jazz pianist, small plane pilot, and scratch golfer. But, except for purgative experiences that may await us after death, things just do not work that way.

King David's cry when confronted with his sins of murder and adultery —"Create in me a clean heart, O God, and put a new and right spirit within me"—is at the heart of his great psalm of repentance and hope. Whether one starts with David or Bill Murray, one discovers that there is more than one approach to sin and imperfection.

For some people, it is enough to know they are "saved." They go on with their lives pretty much unchanged, except for moments of renewed repentance or reconversion. There are also those for whom being justified is not enough. They have the gift of wanting more than escape: they want transformation, want it with a kind of holy desperation. "Blessed are those," Jesus said, "who hunger and thirst after righteousness."

A story from the American Baptist tradition tells of a young man who came to the pastor asking for Baptism. After some conversation, the pastor said the best thing to do would be to go into the church and practice in the baptismal tank. The man agreed. The pastor let him down into the water and pressed down with all his weight. The young man struggled and splashed and gasped. Then the pastor said to the outraged man, "When you want God as much as you just wanted air, I'll be happy to baptize you." The young man was not being asked to create an appetite he did not have, but to clear away the brush enough to understand that the longing he felt for religious assurance was a part of a deeper desire to know and live with God.

What has this to do with Bill Murray and my need for purgation? Neither you nor I will be able to put the world on hold and devote ten thousand Groundhog Days to getting ourselves perfected before resuming our regularly scheduled biographies. We have only ordinary, nonrepeatable days to work out our lives.

But we can rest in God. We can acknowledge that at the bottom of our desires to "be better" is our default desire to live in union with God. Resting in God begins with the simple discipline of remaining aware of God's presence throughout the day, and beginning, a bit at a time, to lean upon that presence, even though stumbling some here and there. Resting in God—at the center of life—not only sheds anxiety but also allows us to experience the freedom to be and do all the things we were made for, one day at a time.

---

## We're All African American This Month
## (Black History Month)

"Today, everybody is Irish." New Yorkers used to say that on Saint Patrick's Day, recognizing important facts about the journey the Irish made through social barriers and celebrating their culture and achievements. People also say there is a sense in which everybody in New York City is Jewish. The culture has been indelibly marked by the presence and accomplishments of the Jews.

February is Black History Month. Are we who are not black ready to say that, in February, we are all African American? That may not come so easily as being Irish for a day. Until we are ready, however, it seems unlikely that America will overcome its endemic racism and that there will truly be an American people.

To embrace the African American experience means at least three things for nonblack people. The first is to own the extent to which the New

World was built on the backs of people torn from their homes: tribal leaders sold them, Muslim slavers captured and warehoused them, nice white Christian Europoids bought, transported, and resold them like cattle.

A tired old lie claims white people did not know better than to treat Africans as subhuman. Of course, they knew; they simply could not afford to let principle interfere with convenience and economic strategy. Oppression is always in denial of the evil it visits on its victims—ask any woman.

To focus on the history of oppression and the debt our society owes to the toil of slaves—and to the toil of wage slaves of all races—is perhaps the easiest task. Somewhat more challenging to white-held stereotypes would be to focus on the tremendous strength and courage that enabled African Americans not only to survive brutality, but to take to the streets to claim a place owed to all Americans. This month we remember not the victims, not only the survivors, but also heroes known and unknown who changed a country.

It is chilling for me to realize that most living Americans do not remember our country before the civil rights era. Consequently, they cannot recall the change that black people made in this culture. Black History Month is important because it is a testimony to strength, courage, and the will to be free in the face of unthinking oppression. It recognizes the effort it took for all the African American scientists, scholars, teachers, parents, and workers just to get to a place where they could make a contribution to a society that was and is slow to recognize a gift when it is given.

The third is probably the most challenging. Northeast Pennsylvania is still predominantly white, though that is changing rapidly. Historians have written how coal, steel, and other large employers encouraged rivalry and distrust between ethnic groups and communities: a divided work force remains weak.

All Americans need to embrace Black History as Our History to enable the changing population of Pennsylvania to once again become an industrial force in this country. The Latino and Asian populations are growing rapidly. Will our region sufficiently overcome its heritage of suspicion and alienation to welcome the contributions all citizens make to the common wealth of the Commonwealth? Until we make the effort to embrace every group's story and accomplishments as part of how we tell the American story and perceive it as America's strength, we will limp as a people.

The myth of the melting pot is long gone: we no longer expect or desire everyone to be somehow the same—which always meant white-acting, Christian-acting—but recognize the fabric of America as a rich tapestry.

When every strand of that tapestry is honored we will be further on the way to becoming one nation.

## We Walk Before We Run (Ash Wednesday)

When I hear anyone lie, my very ordinary background kicks in. Readers of this column know the frequency with which I address public truthfulness as a moral issue. Many may dismiss that morality as "middle-class morality." In ancient Rome, factual honesty was considered a "virtue for tradesmen" but not something patricians need worry about.

A radio host recently explained why her own Jewish tradition's prohibition of blasphemy does not apply to her. The males of royal families in Britain and America have made it clear that for them there are no rules about marital fidelity. Even for some Christian thinkers, ordinary morality is seen as needed perhaps to keep the masses in line, but not for the sophisticated person.

The opposite excuse is often made for people at the other end of the economic scale: that they are too oppressed to be accountable. In one grand patronizing gesture, they too are relieved of moral responsibility. I have more respect for the oppressed than that, and recognize that they have the power to sin as much as anyone else.

I believe that human experience is cumulative. Little honesties add up to honor. Little acts of faithfulness add up to integrity. We walk before we run. Each of us has weaknesses and challenges; each of us knows moments when we lose the struggle and do things that are self-serving or hurtful to others. It is one thing to struggle, even to lose. It is quite another to say there really are no rules for us.

The ability to deceive ourselves is the difference between sin and entrenched evil. We sin all the time, and are sorry and try to live differently. We are evil when we convince ourselves that standards do not apply to us. We then incorporate sin into the way we operate. We have trouble dealing with great social issues because our individual hearts are unconverted.

Most of us are pretty good at recognizing this decay of morality in the culture and in our acquaintances. It doesn't take genius to detect hypocrisy or self-deceit in others. What is more difficult is to get past our own system of defenses and look for the lies we tell ourselves. If we tell ourselves that because we work hard all day we can isolate ourselves from our children or spouse (all of whom have, indeed, had their own day!), we are living a pattern of self-deceit and are being unfaithful. If we think a busy lifestyle excuses us from attending church and encouraging our sisters and brothers with our presence, we are deceiving ourselves. In both cases we hurt others; and our own soul shrivels and contorts.

As Ash Wednesday approaches, many Christians will take a good look inside and go to work on what they see. That has nothing to do with self-hate or depression, both of which keep us from accomplishing anything. It is a matter of recognizing our strength and applying it to the areas of our life that are not reflective of Christ. Christian morality, New Testament morality, is considerably more than the Ten Commandments, but it is not less. We walk before we run.

The function of moral teaching and self-examination is not to make us feel better than others or give us a reason to condemn. Its purpose is to check our self-honesty, our faithfulness in response to God's love. I suspect that none of the above is news. It is a reminder, however, that Lent offers the opportunity to fight sin and develop virtue so that the one person we never feel the need to lie to is our self.

## Changing Our Reality (Lent)

Like many college students, I tended not to do laundry until the pile of clothes in my room developed vital signs of its own or I needed something to wear on a date. I remember being in a rush to get some things clean for an evening out, only to have my heart sink by the sight of three little words on our dorm's laundry room: Out of Order. So polite, so devastating.

Disorder: it's an interesting concept for brokenness, parts not being ordered, not working together in the right way. It has something to tell us during Lent, and explains the one Lenten practice that confuses people more than any other. The "disorder" of which Lent speaks is the somewhat forbidding expression, "disordered affections." Those words simply mean that love can get out of hand.

Those of us who fight a lifetime battle with weight know there are days when we love carbohydrates more than exercise, the comfort of food more than the prospect of long and healthy life. There are people who dispro-portionately desire ambition, comfort, possessions, or prestige. Sometimes this is cute; puppy love, or parking one's first car across two spaces at the farthest point in the parking lot, doesn't last forever. Lent is the time to ask bigger questions: Are there things we love too much?

The most misunderstood idea about Lent is that of giving things up. While many meanings have been attached to the practice, the root idea is freedom, choosing to put things back in order. I am a slave to whatever I cannot do without. If life is unthinkable without television, shopping, or chocolate, I am not free.

Up to this point most people might agree. If we go one step beyond this, however, and ask what are the nonphysical things that we are slaves to, hackles rise. Can we get through a day without complaining about other people? It's awfully comforting to emphasize the shortcomings of others; it can even make one feel superior. Can we get through the day without having to have power over others—letting our loved ones be themselves? People who are embarrassed by their parents have not yet become their own person.

Psychological or spiritual disorder of the affections puts our feeling good, valuable, or powerful above the welfare, dignity, or freedom of others. We destroy community. This can't be fixed by giving up a candy bar. But whether we adjust our eating habits or adjust what we allow ourselves to say about other things or people, by breaking free of disordered affections, our reality changes. The idea that God is with us as we break free and pass from one mode of being to another is as old as the Exodus, and gives us courage to take the first step to freedom.

Biting the tongue as soon as you feel the urge to complain about the turkeys who plague your life may turn out to be a moment of liberation: they aren't running your life. Have you ever had an idea mistaken for a joke? I have twice suggested to church groups recently that the ideal thing to give up in Lent is complaining. The prolonged laughter that followed my suggestion would have done a comic proud. Perhaps I need to work on my timing. "But seriously, folks," what would life be like if we simply determined not to complain, if we worked with what is, emphasizing the positive and the potential? It's only six weeks.

## Giving Up Victimhood for Lent

The Devil made me do it. For most of us, that expression is a joke or a child's evasion of responsibility. It is worth thinking about, however, as February brings us Lent's call to look within ourselves. Who are the "devils" we invoke to avoid responsibility?

Adam blamed Eve; Eve blamed the snake. Some people blame psychological "addictions" or other boutique disabilities. Others blame their parents, their bosses, their relative wealth or poverty, their supposed experience of victimhood or oppression.

Unprincipled defense lawyers and well-paid expert witnesses of the type lawyers consider prostitutes argue that nobody is ever at fault except, perhaps, those who seek justice. Something in us would rather establish convoluted theories or complicated patterns of alibi, rather than simply say, "I was wrong. I'm sorry. I'll try to do better." From cop-out to perjury, human nature seeks any tool to avoid taking responsibility—and deprives itself of grace and growth.

There may be otherwise normal people who are so ill that they have no power to avoid taking the first drink, the first snort, using the first credit card, or whatever. I haven't met any.

For very complex reasons we may construct patterns of behavior that feel good or at least stop the pain. When the patterns are entrenched enough to be habits or ways of life, we feel out of control. Then, of course, we want to say we are not responsible for what we do. But the pattern began with an act, a decision, a curiosity, a response to a hunger or a hurt.

Perhaps a mother, a fifth-grade teacher, or a physical pain had something to do with a person's establishing a pattern of destructive behavior. Those outside "devils" were the stimulus. Adults, however, have the ability to examine what patterns of response they allowed to develop or stay in place.

A fifty-year-old huffily clinging to a nine-year-old's behaviors is pitiful. A fifty-year-old taking responsibility to learn new patterns of behavior is noble and courageous. There can be little grace where people insist they don't need any.

Every one of us has a set of hurts, habits, and vulnerabilities that make us more likely than some other people to commit bad behaviors of one kind or another. That is merely sin, and is fairly easily dealt with. When we lie to ourselves about it, we risk becoming worse than sick; we risk becoming evil, and that is hard to deal with.

The self-examination of Lent is an opportunity to risk peeling the onion of the layers of convenient half-truths, evasions, and self-serving distortions beneath bad behavior. Though this may involve the companionship or guidance of a trusted friend or professional, it is work no one can do for us.

"Dead to sin" is a New Testament expression for studied insensitivity to our own special pleading—alive to the life of strength and grace abundantly available only to those who admit they need it.

I pray that all of us may have a happy and arduous Lent.

## Sorting for Sameness (Lent)

I remember well when a very bright young man from the south side of Bethlehem came to study at Yale University's divinity school. He did not speak or dress like most of the preppie population, and he had somewhere formed the habit of questioning what everybody else took for granted. To watch his treatment was an amazing study in how illiberal a professedly liberal community could be.

But this is not an Ivy-League problem alone. There still are Roman Catholics who, despite the clear teaching of Vatican II, speak of fellow Christians as belonging to "other religions." There still are Protestants who believe that Roman Catholicism is an intentional conspiracy to deny people the light of the gospel and raise money for the pope.

Judaism and Islam also provide their own examples of sectarian thinking. In American history we are aware of some white people who considered black people "soulless." The compliment has been repaid by those in this century who speak consistently of "white devils." For just two more examples, ask some French people to describe the English national character, or some Japanese to describe the Korean, or vice versa. The results are just as chilling.

Ideology, race, nationality—matters of biology or culture—can become the basis or the excuse for the truly obscene. Our century started with the Turkish extermination of some ten million Armenians, moved to the Stalinist killing of thirty million Ukrainians, saw the Nazi slaughter of six million Jews plus unnumbered Gypsies, homosexuals, and political dissidents. Genocide continues.

On the less overtly violent level, cultural, religious, and class issues support systems of oppression in every country, including our own. Almost any evil can be justified if "they" are different.

When you look at or describe other people, do you make it a point to concentrate on sameness or difference? The answer to that question may determine a good deal of your behavior. Listen to yourself and those around you for a day. The point becomes clear. Sorting for difference is a whole lot easier than sorting for sameness or evoking empathy or understanding.

In the Jewish Scriptures, the story of Abraham and Sarah begins after the scattering of the nations. In a chaotic and hostile world Abraham is called out to bring the world a blessing. The Christian Scriptures describe the work of Christ as "breaking down the dividing wall of hostility." St.

Paul's ministry largely involved transforming a local sect into an international community, shaking some people's deepest beliefs about human relations.

For Christians today, the call of Abraham provides the model. The teaching and work of Jesus provide a way. It is up to us to do the sweaty work of bridging the gaps or destroying the walls between people. People who try this way discover common cause with people of many backgrounds and beliefs. The risk begins to be rewarded.

The path to community is by no means easy, and can cost ridicule or even death. On a simpler level, the cost may be a tremendous shift in attitude as I discover that I can respect another person without abandoning my own principles and beliefs. Probably the most important thing I was ever told in my religious formation was, "Paul, always remember that the other person holds their beliefs with the same degree of integrity as you do yours."

As Lent wears on, I see more clearly the necessity for individuals and, through them, of our culture to become less defensive, more interested in finding commonality with those who might be initially perceived as different or a threat. There is really nothing to lose, and a great deal to gain.

## The Passion of the Christ:
## You Could Make a Movie Out of It (Holy Week)

The familiar gospels sprang from compact stories of Jesus' death. They grew as more stories were remembered and recorded. You could make a movie out of how Jesus confronted and defeated death. What would your movie emphasize?

It's hard to put the main character in a box. Sometimes tender, sometimes poetic, sometimes speaking judgment, sometimes downright apocalyptic, driven by a vision of the reign of God, he fits in nobody's pocket. Headed for trouble, he speaks of it as his greatest accomplishment. As an adult, I've struggled with his story for more than forty years (enough time to have reached any other promised land), but Jesus the Christ eludes the grasp of being figured out, possessed, domesticated. I have no insight into him that gives me power over him. He cannot be controlled.

It's no surprise that he would be seen as enemy by religious leaders, state officials, and various self-consciously good people. Nobody likes someone who challenges the Way We Do Things. Nobody who makes the elder brother angry is going to be popular.

Christ begins to bear our sins when a friend rats him out for money. Is there any sense of desolation quite like knowing that one you trusted, befriended, loved, or to whom you made yourself in some other way vulnerable has not honored that trust? That some Jews were among the antagonists in the divine drama is irrelevant. What is relevant is that people who thought they stood for good also thought it was acceptable to get rid of one troublemaker in order to protect God and the people. The idea of disposable human life is still around. That other people's lives are not so valuable pervades time and history. Christ before the Sanhedrin is not about Jews, it's about lies people tell themselves when destroying the less powerful.

What about the Romans? They conquered the world without trying to win hearts or minds. They maintained order by systematized brutality that brought a kind of "peace." Ultimate pragmatists, they knew what they had to do—and, having decided to do it, did not leave room for sentiment. Ask the Carthage Chamber of Commerce. In terms of law and order, from a Babylonian original they perfected crucifixion precisely because the whole process, as depicted by Mr. Gibson in such detail, amounted not just to dispatching an undesirable, but the total humiliation, degradation, and reduction to wretchedness of those who were to serve as public warning: resistance is not only useless, it will bring total destruction.

All governments have blood on their hands. Our American self-understanding is that the government reflects our will. Do we see in Jesus before Pilate anything of the complicity of "we the people" in atrocities ancient or modern? Is that too offensive a question to ask in an election year? Have we ever meditated on the photograph of Palestinian teens dancing with joy at the news of 9/11 and asked, why?

My movie is about cosmic and personal forces of evil. The scourging and nailing are a part, not the point. Jesus' suffering and death reveal us for what we are. Pity and horror are appropriate; but if they distract us from the truth that individually and corporately we continue to do the very behaviors that brought the Son of God to horrible death, we will not be changed and the world will not be changed.

My converting moment is that he could pray that God would forgive us. Christ indulges not in victimhood but intercession. The love just never stops. Even the centurion at the foot of the cross gets it. That's what the passion narratives want us to get. By Christ's consistently loving the Creator and the creatures, sin is exposed, love is exalted, and we are invited to look on the one we have pierced. We might as well return to God because his love is just not going to quit.

Gibson's Christ is resurrected with a mean look on his face, striding off perhaps to kick somebody. In the book, however, the Jesus whom the disciples meet after Easter says, "Peace be with you." Endless possibilities.

---

## If Christ Has Not Been Raised (Easter)

A Buddhist master was asked to give a retreat for some Christians. He accepted the challenge, and spent time with the New Testament. He began his remarks by confessing how surprised he was to find out what was in those short documents. "Christianity," he said, "makes sense only if Christ is resurrected. And if he is, your every breath, your posture, and your attitude should show that."

Argument about whether the crucified Jesus was in any sense brought to life is not new, of course, and many people find it difficult or impossible to accept, even if they would like to believe. There are historical arguments that can be mounted to indicate the probability that resurrection took place or not, but those are not conclusive.

Nonetheless, St. Paul threw the gauntlet down in no uncertain way: "If Christ has not been raised," he wrote, "your faith is useless. And of all humans, we believers are the most pitiful." Like our Buddhist master, Paul expressed powerfully the centrality—and the power—of the resurrection.

Paul had a vision of the risen Christ, and knew people who reported their stories of physical encounter with him in ordinary history. I do not know anyone who has had a vision like St. Paul's, and nobody suggests that Jesus walks our earth in the ordinary sense of those words.

How or why does one believe in the continuing presence and power of a living Jesus Christ? The thing I find least helpful is intellectual debate about historical and theological issues: They are more about belief than faith and relationship. They are pointless if there is no living reality behind them.

There are many paths that have led people to Christ. My own mind prefers the simple and direct, and I suggest here three practical things one can do to discover whether Christ is alive.

The first is to set aside a period, perhaps thirty days, in which one will behave as though Christ is there, and that behavior begins with prayer. Prayer is conversation. One speaks and one listens. Sharing life, listening for guidance, thoughtfully offering concerns for the world's needs.

Prayer is, as the saying goes, the practice of the presence of God, living all of one's life in "public," so to speak, and listening, listening for what guidance may come, what perceptions of people and relationships may change.

The second is to alter one's life to include a few hours of service a week, service to the poor or needy. This needs to be done as quietly and directly as possible, a hands-on experience of serving Christ by serving others, looking for his face in theirs. Volunteering at a hospital or soup kitchen, working in a literacy program or after-school tutoring projects are readily available ways to meet Christ in the face of those in need. Loss of self for others, especially in the middle of a "busy" life, is a way to meet the one who was crucified.

A third ingredient in a period of inquiry is to be where faith already is. The weekly gathering of modern-day disciples for praise, prayer, scripture, and sacrament is supplemented by fellowship and the chance to talk with those who are already on the journey. Like its cousins, Christianity is in both the short and long run about being part of a people, a people with identity and mission.

None of this comes as easy answer or quick fix. To find Christ is to go where he went and be where he is. Those places are not always attractive, but they are full of meaning and often bring joy.

For the overwhelming majority of the world's Christians, Easter is a fifty-day celebration, and we are in the middle of it. There is probably no better time to investigate or renew acquaintance with what and whom it celebrates.

---

## When the End Is the Beginning (Easter)

I love and hate films that do not actually end. *Casablanca* is a good example. Problems are resolved and a few of the characters come to know themselves in a new way. As the story ends, however, the main characters go off to face an uncertain future.

Mark seems to have written his Easter Gospel in this way. Before dawn on Sunday, women come to anoint the body of Jesus. The body is not there. A messenger from God tells them that Jesus has risen and will meet the disciples in Galilee. Then, Mark concludes: "So they went out and fled from the tomb, for terror and amazement had seized them; and they said nothing to anyone, for they were afraid."

Mark stops his Gospel virtually in midsentence: "They said nothing to anyone, for they were afraid of . . ." Our translations usually smooth that off for us, but it is as I've described. The reader is left hanging, wondering what will come next. The early hearers and readers of Mark's proclamation knew that he was not so much writing an ending as he was signaling a beginning. What would happen next in the Easter story was up to them. What will happen next for contemporary readers and hearers of this Easter Gospel is up to us.

A few years ago Ronald Scates wrote an article in which he reports that a survey of twenty-six mainline congregations in the United States revealed that the number one reason visitors return and eventually become members is that "the congregation acts like it really believes Jesus is alive through a collective effervescence that pervades everything that is done."

Scates reminds me that technique to get people in the door may be well and good; after people walk through our doors, however, it is not our technique but our faith that matters most if our mission is to be successful. For mission to succeed we need, as individuals and as congregations, to live that effervescence that comes from following a living Lord, an exalted servant.

That, in fact, is why I have a nearly total lack of interest in arguments about whether the tomb was empty or not. I believe it was; even if I did not, however, the "proof" of the resurrection from Easter Monday on lies not in reconstructing a past that cannot be reconstructed. The "proof" is in the present-day encounter Christians have with the person and power of the risen Christ. That is what Mark's Gospel is trying to get me to see in its unfinished Easter story.

One of the most beautifully staged operas I've ever seen was the premiere, some years ago at the Met, of Puccini's *Turandot*. Puccini never finished the opera. When he died in 1924, his work was reverently finished by friends from his notes.

At its Italian La Scala premiere in 1926, *Turandot* was conducted by Arturo Toscanini. One of the stories told about this premiere is that when Toscanini came to the last passage Puccini had written, the conductor lowered his baton. Turning to the audience, he said through tears: "This is where the master ends."

Then he raised the baton and said: "This is where the friends continue." He went on to what has to have been one of the greatest premieres in musical history. Easter is a springboard into God's future. It is as though today we paradoxically remember tomorrow. Jesus is going on ahead of us. We have the master's notes. In fact, we have the risen master with us. May we, his friends, continue the story.